MW01016589

wishing you all the success
in the world.

Patrick

The more you get out of this book, the closer you'll get to success!

I don't want you to read for the sake of reading—I'd like you to read to understand and learn. I know that when I read a book from cover to cover, I only retain about 20 percent of the content once I'm done with it. A book contains too much information for me to understand everything the first time I read it.

Let's pause for a moment and get some firm ground under our feet. One reading comprehension study says that readers retains 60% of what they read, but I beg to differ. If the reading material is in story form, the 60% is probably accurate. But if it's instructional material, the average reader might retain 40% or less, depending on their interest in the subject matter. Why? Because the mind can only consume small meals at a time or it gets indigestion. Don't read for the sake of reading. Read to understand and learn.

It is a proven fact that a person must be exposed to the same material three times before they can fully retain it. The first time, the reader gets acquainted with new material and soon forgets it. If he reads the same material a second time, he recognizes a familiarity with the subject, but he still forgets it. The third time he reads it, he thinks, "Aha! Now I understand that," and he puts it into practice. However, if he doesn't continue to put it into practice, he'll still forget it.

So I've developed a different reading habit. Each time I read something interesting in a book, I take notes or mark the page with a sticky note so I can reread those sections later. I can only retain something by reading it a few times. I prefer this approach instead of reading the entire book a few times. I encourage you to use a similar approach while reading this book so you can get the most out of it.

Reading tips to help with your comprehension

- ▶ Highlight the areas that most apply to you, or underline them, or put sticky notes on the pages. At a later time, you can leaf through the book and easily find the places you marked.

- ▶ Read each chapter as often as you need to understand all its contents. If needed, read a chapter twice before going on to the next one.

- ▶ As you read my suggestions, ask yourself how you can apply them to your life. And, at every opportunity possible, apply them in your day-to-day life activities to see what results they produce.

- ▶ Once a week, revisit your highlighted text or sticky notes, and reread this information to refresh your memory.

This would be a good time to go get that pen, highlighter, sticky notes, or whatever you want to use.

FINDING YOUR ROAD TO SUCCESS

Patrick Daniel, CA

PDCA PUBLISHING

PDCA PUBLISHING, a division of PDCA Consultant Inc.
151 Albareto, Dollard-Des-Ormeaux, Quebec
Canada, H9G-2Y8

Finding Your Road To Success
Copyright © 2010 Patrick Daniel

All rights reserved. No part of this book may be reproduced by any mechanical, photographic, or electronic process, or in the form of a phonographic recording; nor may it be stored in a retrieval system, transmitted, or otherwise to be copied for public or private use—other than for "fair use" as brief quotations embodied in articles or reviews—without prior written permission of the publisher.

This publication is designed to provide competent and reliable information regarding the subject matter covered. However, it is sold with the understanding that the author and publisher are not engaged in rendering legal, financial, psychological, or other professional advice. Laws and practices often vary from province to province, or state to state, and if legal or other expert assistance is required, the services of a professional should be sought. The author and publisher specifically disclaim any liability that is incurred from the use of application of the contents of this book.

Every effort has been made to ensure no existing copyrighted material has been used in this book. In the event of a question as to the use of any copyrighted material, we will be pleased to make the required corrections in any future printings.

For information regarding special discounts for bulk purchases, please contact PDCA Publishing at
bulk@findingyourroadtosuccess.com.

Cover design by **Beckii Adel**

Printed in USA
First printing

ISBN 978-0-9867060-0-4

This book is dedicated
to my departed father

DANIEL HANNA DANIEL DANIEL

who has truly inspired
me to be the best that
I can be.

In Christ you believed and with him you rest.

Contents

ACKNOWLEDGMENTS

You are holding this book today because of the many people who have helped me enjoy success in my own life. I'd like to give my heartfelt thanks and gratitude to

- **God**, the source of all fulfillments, who makes all things possible. Thanks for giving me the strength to help me help myself, and for carrying me through the rough times. I thank you for giving us your only son **Jesus**, and for sending **Blessed Mother Marie-Alphonsine** as my guardian angel for each step I take in life. I love you and without you I would not be anything. You are my rock!

- My beautiful wife **Sandra**, who brings me much joy and happiness each day. Thank you for your comments and support over the years that I've been writing this book. My journey has been a success because you have been a part of my life. Thanks for believing in me.

- Both my parents. **Mom**, you have always been by my side encouraging me to reach out for my dreams. I am truly blessed and proud to have you as my mother. **Dad**, not a day goes by without me thinking about you. I hope I have become the man you would have liked me to be. Can't wait to see you again. Love you both!

- My brothers, **John** and **Michael**. Not only are you my brothers, but you're my best friends. Thanks for all the special moments we've spent together. You have made my journey through life so much more enjoyable. Without you, success would not be possible.

- **Pixie**, our dog, who brings unconditional love and happiness into our home. Thanks for cheering us up when we are feeling down.

- My dear **friends**, who are way too many to list. Thanks for all the great experiences and memories we've shared together.

- My editor, **Linda**. I was nervous in having you mess with my book, but I really should not have worried. You just made my book better. I appreciate all that you have done for me.

PREFACE

In this section you will learn that:

✓ If you expect to be successful, you'll be successful. If you expect to fail, you probably will.

✓ You're in control of everything around you.

✓ The road to success is a journey, and you need a map.

You may know the story about four people named **Everybody**, **Somebody**, **Anybody**, and **Nobody**. There was an important job to be done and Everybody was sure that Somebody would do it. Anybody could have done it, but Nobody did it. Somebody got angry because it was Everybody's job. Everybody thought Anybody could do it, but Nobody realized that Everybody wouldn't do it. It ended up that Everybody

> "The superior man blames himself. The inferior man blames others."
> – *Don Shula*

blamed Somebody when Nobody did what Anybody could have done.

Does this sound familiar? This is the story of our current society because, sadly, we live in a world where we all expect someone else to do our job, and yet we claim that no one could get the job done better than us. And when something goes wrong, we start to play the blame game—it's never our own fault and always someone else's. No one takes responsibility and, unfortunately, no one succeeds.

This book will help you to realize that you're the biggest obstacle to your success. If you expect to be successful, you'll be successful. But if you expect to fail, you probably will. My hope is that by reading this book, you will learn that before someone else can start to believe in you, you have to believe in yourself. You have to take matters into your own hands, for you and only you have what it takes to succeed. Others can't do it for you! If you feel that your life is not going as you planned, it's most likely your fault. Don't forget, the biggest obstacle to achieving your success is *you*.

The road to success is a journey, and you need a map for that journey that shows a clear final destination. Without a final destination, how do you know where you need to go? You don't. You'll just be going around in circles not really knowing what direction your life needs to take. But drawing up your life's map and pinpointing your final destination doesn't mean that everything in life will come easily. You'll encounter obstacles—potholes, closed roads, construction, accidents, detours, and one-way streets. As you encounter each obstacle, keep in mind that there's always an alternative route that you can take to put you back on the road that leads to your success.

I wrote this book as a personal mission; it's something that I have been thinking about for a few years. The idea came from friends and co-workers, who often seek my advice and opinion. I seem to be "the guy" who everyone comes to for advice—they are always interested in what I would do if I were them, or how I "did it," or my opinion on what they should do. Since I'm the go-to person, I figured that I must be doing something right.

> "It is our attitude at the beginning of a difficult task which, more than anything else, will affect its successful outcome."
> – *William James*

Most of my writing reflects my experiences, observations, and personal views and thoughts. You may find yourself disagreeing with things I say, because what works for me may not work for you. If you find that you strongly disagree with what I say, I encourage you to write to me (see my contact information at the end of this book). We all grow and better ourselves through sharing different views, opinions, and experiences, and I'm sure I can learn many things from you.

As you read further, I hope to spark in you a deeper awareness of the powers that you possess. Once you have that, you'll be able to start altering yourself and making the necessary changes to the way you think, the way you deal with obstacles, and the way you feel. You'll notice how these changes start to affect your attitude in a positive, constructive way, and finding your road to success becomes easy.

The Donkey in the Well

One day a farmer's donkey fell down into a well. The animal cried piteously for hours as the farmer tried to figure out what to do.

Finally he decided since the animal was old, and the well needed to be covered up anyway, it just wasn't worth it to retrieve the donkey. So, the farmer invited all his neighbors to come over and help him. They all grabbed shovels, and began to shovel dirt into the well.

All the other farm animals were very upset about this, because the donkey was their friend. But they discovered there was nothing they could do to help him.

At first, when the donkey realized what was happening, he cried horribly. Then, to everyone's amazement, he quieted down. A few shovel loads later, the farmer finally looked down the well, and was astonished at what he saw.

With every shovel of dirt that hit his back, the donkey was doing something amazing. He would shake it off, and take a step up on the dirt as it piled up. As the farmer's neighbors continued to shovel dirt on top of the animal, he would shake it off and take a step up. Pretty soon, everyone was amazed as the donkey stepped up over the edge of the well, and trotted off!

http://www.donkeystory.com/

Life is going to shovel all kinds of dirt on you. But each trouble can be a stepping stone with the right attitude and roadmap. What happens to you isn't nearly as important as how you react to it. You can get out of the deepest wells just by not giving up! When you find yourself in a well, shake it off, and take a step up!

Chapter 1

INTRODUCTION

In this section you will learn about:

✓ Who I am.

✓ The game of life, in which you need a bit of an edge to separate you from the rest of the pack.

At a young age, I knew that in the game of life, everyone is playing the same game with the same deck of cards. It's like a blackjack table at a casino. Everyone is at the same table, with the same dealer, playing with the same deck. Most of us lose every now and then, but in each round there's one person who wins. To me, losing at blackjack is a metaphor for losing in the game of life, which for me would be finding myself stuck with a 25-year mortgage and running the rat race trying to survive in a very debt-intense world. There's nothing wrong with losing at the blackjack table. After all, the odds are against us and everyone loses at some point, so it doesn't make us losers—it makes us normal. But that's exactly what I didn't want to be. I've always wanted to be *better* than normal, which to me, was my measurement of success.

Reaching my "above average" goal

Early in my career, I began to use most of the money that I earned to get it to work for me. I invested in real estate and the financial markets, which produce passive income. This passive income became the main source of funding for much of my living and entertainment expenses (I provide some tips on how to best manage your money in Chapter 6.)

By the time I was 31, my net worth was more than that of the average person aged 65 years or older, according to American and Canadian statistics. I was making good money, I had no debt, and I had no mortgage on the house I owned. (This last point is particularly important, since a mortgage hurts you financially over many years.) I'm very good at handling my

> *"A successful man is one who can lay a firm foundation with the bricks others have thrown at him."*
> *– David Brinkley*

financial affairs—I have five credit cards with a combined limit of over $40,000 but my total balance owing each month is *zero.*

You may think that my life must revolve around work so that I can make as much money as possible, but that is not the case. My success is not only financial, and there's more to me than just work. I travel frequently in the wonderful company of my wife Sandra—to date I have visited over 20 countries.

When I'm not traveling, I love spending time with my family and friends. There's no one more important in my life than my family—my wife, mother, brothers, cousins, aunts, uncles, and everyone else related to me by blood or by marriage. I love spending time with them and try to do it as often as possible.

My friends are definitely next on my list, since I also consider them family. I truly believe that I have the best family and friends in the world.

I volunteer regularly. I've been part of the Big Brothers program since 2002 and enjoy spending time with my Little Brother. I also like to

NET WORTH - Median in US $ *	
Males and Females, all ages	
Less than 25	$ 1,475
25 to 34	$ 8,525
35 to 44	$ 51,575
45 to 54	$ 98,350
55 to 64	$ 180,125
65 and older	$ 232,000

* Findings according to CNN Net Worth Calculator

NET WORTH - Median in Cdn $ **	
Males, all ages	
Less than 35	$ 28,203
35 to 44	$ 150,225
45 to 54	$ 273,483
55 to 64	$ 448,795
65 and older	$ 405,000
Females, all ages	
Less than 35	$ 9,900
35 to 44	$ 96,856
45 to 54	$ 178,650
55 to 64	$ 345,877
65 and older	$ 204,833

** Findings from survey performed by Statistics Canada in 2005

volunteer my time at homeless shelters serving meals, handing out food baskets, and fundraising to purchase Christmas toys for underprivileged children. You might also find me on the streets talking to the homeless and buying them sandwiches.

Last but not least, I dedicate some time for prayer each day. I am a practicing Catholic and enjoy visiting the church frequently to light candles and pray for my family, friends, and all the suffering people in the world. I've even had the opportunity to volunteer for Pope Benedict XVI during his visit to Lourdes, France, in 2008. Being able to serve over 150,000 pilgrims and seeing the Pope in person was one of the greatest experiences of my life. It was absolutely priceless.

> *"Success doesn't come to you. You go to it."*
> *– Marva Collins*

These are things I hold dear to my heart, and I always make sure that I make enough time for them. They are what make my life "above average" in ways that have nothing to do with making money and being successful financially. Life is great!

So what's the secret?

Why am I so happy with my life? It's simple—I have discovered the secret to my success. And with this success comes the feeling of great pride—pride in who I am and what I've become, pride in what I've achieved so far in my personal and professional life, pride in my beautiful and supportive wife, and pride in my family and friends.

To me, success doesn't mean being extremely wealthy—as I have already said, it's more being financially better than average. So, my goal is to make enough money to be comfortable, to be able to travel at least twice a year, and to be around for my kids without having to spend all my time at work trying to provide for them. I still haven't achieved all of these goals, but I'm definitely on the right path.

The goal of this book is to share with you how I got to where I am—how I make sure that I'm winning the game of life, and the day-to-day habits that I have incorporated into my life. I also share how I worked on changing my attitude into a more positive one, no matter what happens in my life.

I explain what my dreams and goals were, and how I mapped my life to achieve them. Without my roadmap, I'd be lost—I wouldn't know where to go. My map includes how important money is for me. To prepare the map, I had to get a good understanding of how much money I needed, how to save it, and how to stretch it to the maximum. I also had to include the other aspects of my life in my roadmap.

Once I got an understanding of all of these facets of my ideal life, I was able to unlock the secret to my success. I finally knew where I had to be to achieve my success. From there, it was a matter of execution. With my map in hand and the secret to my success unlocked, I was ready to begin my journey.

Now it's time for you to unlock the secret of your success and let *your* journey begin!

Before my map began

To help you better understand my route, where I've been and where I currently am, let me tell you a bit about myself and my life. A little later in the book, I'll tell you where I would like to be in the future, as I still have many goals that I would like to achieve as I grow older.

Here is my story to date …

I was born in Saudi Arabia in 1976 to wonderful parents—my father moved to Saudi Arabia in the 1970s to open a computer company, and my mother stayed home to take care of three boys, me being the middle child.

Since I'm from a Middle Eastern background, you might expect me to have a traditional Arabic name, but I don't and neither do my brothers. My parents wanted us to travel and make the most of the world, so they gave us common names that were easy to pronounce and would not expose us to discrimination: John, Michael and, of course, Patrick. Since English is the international language of business, my brothers and I

> *"Health is the greatest gift, contentment the greatest wealth, faithfulness the best relationship."*
> *– Buddha*

were sent to American and British schools to learn the language, and we learned the Arabic language at home.

Traveling was my family's favorite pastime, and we often spent summers and holidays with family in different countries. After nine years in Saudi Arabia enjoying the frequent traveling, a good English education, and the hot days in the desert on the weekends, my family opted for a change. In 1985, my mother, my brothers, and I moved to the European island of Cyprus, while my father remained in Saudi Arabia to run his company. He came to visit us at least once a month.

Cyprus was completely different than Saudi Arabia. As non-Muslims living in Saudi Arabia, safety was always a concern, and we were unable to practice being Christians openly. But now my mother felt liberated. She could leave the house without covering up with a veil each time, attend church and drive herself around, all of which were forbidden in Saudi Arabia. Cyprus had a lot to offer in terms of lifestyle, freedom and safety.

My brothers and I were at the age when we needed to start socializing, and Cyprus let us do that. It was ideal because my parents did not have to worry about us when we were outside playing and making many new friends. We went to a private British school and met lots of new people. What great memories I have of Cyprus and, looking back now, Cyprus was like paradise!

But in 1987 everything changed. My father passed away from cancer at the age of 36 in London, England. This devastated the family and posed a big challenge for my mother, who was left alone to raise three devil kids between the ages of 8 and 14.

One of my father's dreams was to see at least one of his sons obtain a university degree, and my mother decided to honor this dream. With a courageously strong will and resolve, she packed everything up and moved us from Cyprus to Montreal, Canada in the summer of 1988. She did this against the will of both my father's family and her own family, who wanted her to move to either Jordan or France so that they could help her raise us. My mother, being strong and independent, stuck true to the Canada plan by having my paternal grandmother come with us.

And so, a new life in Canada began. Everything was different and new—the country, the people, the school, the house, the language, and the culture. I had skipped two grades in school, but found myself in trouble a few months later when I was forced to continue my schooling in French, as that was a requirement for all new immigrants to Montreal.

> *"Wherever you go, no matter what the weather, always bring your own sunshine."*
> *– Anthony J. D'Angelo*

Now in a French school, I watched my grades slip drastically, and ended up having to repeat tenth grade twice. Times were hard for me but I wasn't the only one experiencing difficulties in this new life. My mother, widowed and wanting to provide the most for her children and mother-in-law, was running out of money quickly.

She was forced to get a job, so she went back to school and got her real estate license.

For my mother and I, getting back on our feet was hard and took time, but it ended on a positive note. My mother became one of the most successful real estate agents in the area, and I got to learn a new language. Although studying in French was difficult, I made it through high school and was accepted into an English-language college in the commerce program, thanks to my strong mathematics grades and a well-written letter explaining why my high school grades were so poor. From there, I obtained my university bachelor's degree in commerce in 1998 and a graduate degree in accounting in 2000. Later that year, I wrote and passed the national Canadian chartered accountant exam on my first attempt. I was the second of my father's sons to achieve his dream of us getting a university degree.

The game begins in earnest

As I approached the end of my university studies, I knew that the day for me to find my first real job was quickly approaching. My game of life, in which I had to play at the same table and with the same set of rules as everyone around me, was about to start. I knew that I needed a bit of an edge, something that would set me apart from the rest of the pack. I was determined to be the winner on the blackjack table, so I needed something to tip the odds in my favor. My grades weren't spectacular so I couldn't use them to my advantage, and in terms of contacts in the work force, I had none! So how was I to make it in such a demanding, aggressive world? After some time and much thought, it occurred to me that I (me, myself) had all the power to make things different. I had to work on myself to make things work in my favour. My attitude needed to change and I had to think of things differently. No more complaining. No more following the crowd. I had to separate myself from the pack or I would find myself in the same boat as everyone else. I would be normal! And that was my biggest fear.

One of my dreams while I was an accounting student was to work for PricewaterhouseCoopers, one of the biggest accounting firms in the world. Although I had good grades in university, they didn't meet the minimum requirements to work for PricewaterhouseCoopers. I was disappointed but I did not let it discourage me.

I ended up starting my career as an external auditor with a smaller accounting firm. Fresh out of school, I was eager to learn and very dedicated to my work. I asked my supervisors a lot of questions because I wanted to know everything about how they did things and why they did them. Within six months my responsibilities were increased to those of a senior auditor, which generally takes two years to accomplish. A few months later, I advanced my career by joining my dream firm,

> *"Dream as if you'll live forever, live as if you'll die today."*
> *– James Dean*

PricewaterhouseCoopers. I felt like I was on top of the world.

Over the years to come, my career excelled to the point where I was experienced enough to start my own accounting practice and become my own boss. My accounting firm specializes in providing services related to an American securities law (called the Sarbanes-Oxley Act) of 2002.

In addition, I wanted to try something outside the financial world. I opened a theater production company with the intention of reviving a great British comedy television show from the 70s called *Mind Your Language*. I also got involved with the start-up of two other companies, one that uses laser technology to engrave three-dimensional pictures of people in a crystal cube, and another that sells various products online.

Working on companies outside the financial world was very challenging and very rewarding. I was able to rise successfully to some challenges, which made me feel great, while I learned great lessons from some other challenges. I discovered that the hardest thing about owning a few companies simultaneously was that I was not able to devote my full attention to all of them. Within a year or so, I finally realized that my strength was in the field of accounting, not theater or crystal products, so I refocused all my energy on providing accounting services. I was back on focus. I found my success, I enjoy my life, and I live very happily.

Chapter 2

DECIDE WHAT SUCCESS MEANS TO YOU

In this section you will learn that:

✓ Only you can define your own success.

✓ True success is a well-balanced package, not just based on money and fame.

✓ Everyone needs to define their Ultimate Success.

At age 4 success is . . . not peeing in your pants.
At age 12 success is . . . having friends.
At age 16 success is . . . having a driver's license.
At age 20 success is . . . having sex.
At age 35 success is . . . having money.

At age 50 success is . . . having money.
At age 60 success is . . . having sex.
At age 70 success is . . . having a driver's license.
At age 75 success is . . . having friends.
At age 80 success is . . . not peeing in your pants.

I n the game called *Success*, you begin on square one. You and your game piece then take a long journey—one that lasts a lifetime. The board is a maze, so you must navigate by making a series of choices. Along the way, you encounter many thrills, obstacles, setbacks and surprises.

The problem with the *Success* game is that none of the players are born with a set of instructions for how to play. The game is very complicated, and when you're in the maze it's difficult to determine where the final square—what I call Ultimate Success—is on the board. Life would be so much easier if we had the instructions!

Since we don't come with instructions at birth, our responsibility is to figure out how to play *Success*. We must devise our own set of instructions, and clear objectives on how to win.

Society's definition of success

Let's begin by discussing how our society defines success. My interpretation of society's definition is pretty simple—you're considered successful if you can answer yes to at least two of the following questions:

$ Do you own a big house?

$ Do you drive an expensive sports car?

$ Are you an Ivy League graduate with a master's degree?

$ Are you a doctor or lawyer?

$ Are you a millionaire?

$ Are you famous?

$ Are you the CEO of a multi-billion-dollar company?

As you can see, society's definition of success doesn't take happiness, family, good health, religious faith, or good ethical values into consideration. It's simply based on education, money, fame, and material possessions. But does all this really matter to you? To feel successful, do you need any or all of them?

Sadly, the media and people around us would have us believe that money is the most important element for success. But I don't agree with many of our society's beliefs. When I look at famous actors and actresses, who have lots of money and all the fame one can dream of, I question whether they are truly successful, because they are missing some elements of success that I consider important.

> *"Don't confuse fame with success. Madonna is one; Helen Keller is the other".*
> *– Erma Bombeck*

I can't deny that their achievement is a success story, but are fame and fortune all that are needed to be really successful? How about their turbulent personal lives, with multiple divorces and bad habits such as alcohol abuse? Shouldn't those factors be considered in the evaluation of success? Are they surrounded by love and support? Do they have strong family ties? Is there any happiness in their lives? Most importantly, do *they* feel successful with their lives? I don't know the answers to these questions, but I do know that I would not trade places with most of them even for ten million dollars.

My definition of success

You may see nothing wrong with society's definition of success, but to me it is only a small piece of the pie. Money and a good job simply aren't enough for me to feel successful. I started to realize this in the beginning of my career when I was working hard trying to make as much money as I could. The money was coming in, but the harder I worked, the less happy I felt. I missed my friends and family, and something just didn't feel right. How could I be working hard and making money but be feeling miserable? That's when I realized that I was trying to satisfy society's definition of success, not my own. I started to develop my own definition of success—one that includes the small things in life that make me most happy, rather than just what society expects of me.

Since then, I haven't allowed society to impose its definition of success on me because, in all honesty, society doesn't know me or what my pleasures are. I refuse to let society push me in the wrong direction. I've never been the type to let others tell me what to do—as a child, I challenged my parents' authority when I disagreed with their methods, opinions, or disciplinary actions. Ironically, most of these instances resulted in me getting a spanking! But despite the punishments I received, these early experiences have served me well. I still stand up for myself when I truly believe in something, regardless of the consequences.

How do I figure out what success means for me? It's pretty simple: I have to know what truly makes me happy. When I say "me," I really do mean me—not my brothers, my parents, or my friends. No one knows me better than I do, so this task can't be done by anyone but me. Nor can I define success for anyone else,

> "*If your success is not on your own terms, if it looks good to the world but does not feel good in your heart, it is not success at all.*"
> – *Anna Quindlen*

because I don't know them the way they know themselves. What I consider as being a success may not suit someone else.

Success takes a step at a time

As a kid, I always loved playing with Lego. In fact, I still enjoy building things with Lego. A few years ago, I underwent laser eye surgery to correct my vision. The doctor's orders were not to watch television, read, or use a computer for a few days following the surgery. In need of some entertainment, I bought a kit for building a Lego motorcycle that had over a thousand pieces. It kept me busy for several days, during which I started to realize that success is very much like a Lego set.

A Lego kit is comprised of many pieces, some big and some small. At first, you can't imagine how they will all fit together, and the task before you seems very complicated. But once you start to put the pieces together with the step-by-step instructions, your creation slowly starts to take shape and becomes something recognizable.

Each piece that I snapped into place brought me one step closer to finishing my motorcycle, and each piece made the motorcycle more recognizable. About a week later, when I finally placed my last piece, I achieved my final success: a big, beautiful model of a Harley Davidson motorcycle.

So what does Lego have to do with success? Each day in life is like a single piece. If you use up your day correctly, it brings you one step closer to your goal, your success. Some days have big achievements while others have small ones, just as the Lego box has some big pieces and some small. But here is the key to it all: the step-by-step instructions. They gave me a roadmap to follow on the journey that began with a thousand disorganized pieces and ended with a unified whole that gave me a feeling of accomplishment and satisfaction. I realized that if I hadn't had the instructions, it would have been virtually impossible for me to build the motorcycle accurately. The instructions were the key!

The game of *Success* also needs step-by-step instructions. As you'll read later on in this chapter, the instruction sheet—your roadmap—becomes one of your most valuable possessions, because it shows you the correct path to follow to reach each success in life on your way to achieving your Ultimate Success.

Success is a feeling

When thinking or talking about your success, be careful with the words you choose. If I said "I *am* successful," others could disagree. They might not understand that success means more to me than earning money and having prestige. They could compare me to someone like Bill Gates, and argue that I'm not particularly successful. But if I say "I *feel* successful," that changes everything. Nobody else can tell you how you feel, challenge your statement, or prove you wrong. Many will try to rob you of this great feeling because they're envious, but as long as you don't let them get to you, your feelings are untouchable. This is why it's important that you and only you define your success. You're the only person with control of your feelings, and you're the one who knows what it takes to *feel* successful.

Successes can be large or small

Before you begin the task of figuring out what success really means to you, it's important to remember that when we talk about success, we're not talking only about something huge in your life. Even the smallest accomplishments can be considered successes.

For example, let's say that one of your goals is to get your university diploma. The journey to achieve this success is comprised of many small steps, each of which can be seen as a sub-success. Each homework assignment that you complete is a success. Each quiz and exam you pass is a success. Each midterm and final examination you pass is a success, as is each course you pass. Passing *all* your courses is also a success. And once you've done that, guess what? You have achieved one of your success criteria by obtaining your diploma.

As you can see, your achievement starts with one sub-success, which leads to another, and yet another, until you obtain your diploma. Each step along the way—the small ones and the larger ones—is a success towards your end goal. But not all sub-successes are necessarily needed to achieve a success. An important point to remember is that if you fail at one of the steps at the sub-success level, it doesn't mean you can't achieve your final goal. Just because you do poorly on an assignment does not mean that

> *"No matter how far you fall down, you gotta be ready to stand up."*
> *– Akon*

you'll fail your final examination. Giving up shouldn't be an option—you just have to change your strategy. Take that failure and learn from it. Figure out why you did poorly and then take action to make sure you don't repeat the mistakes. Maybe you didn't dedicate enough time for studying, or maybe you simply didn't understand the lesson and need to revisit parts of the course. Not all sub-successes are required for you to reach your ultimate goal, and not all failures mean that you can't achieve that goal.

What's the difference between success and sub-success? They are the same, except a success will most likely be made up of many sub-successes. When I mention success in this book, I mean everything from small sub-successes to major successes that take many years to achieve.

Your definition is unique to you

Everyone has different desires in life, so no one can define success for you—you have to do it yourself.

Just to show how we are all different from one another, here's a partial list of all the pieces that will need to fit together for me to achieve my Ultimate Success goal. As you read through the list, think about how your criteria compare to mine.

- ▶ At a young age, one of my desires was to make a million dollars by the time I reached 30 years old.

- ▶ I wanted to obtain a graduate degree in accounting.

- ▶ I wanted to be married by the time I was 30.

- ▶ I want to be a parent by the time I'm 35.

- ▶ I always wanted to see the Pope in person.

- ▶ I try to devote as much of my time to volunteering as possible, because I'd like to make a difference in people's lives.

- Taking a vacation twice a year to travel is a must for me.

- I want to be semi-retired before I'm 40.

- I'd like to spend part of my children's younger years at home raising them, so I don't miss their growing up.

- I'd like to spend part of my life living and working in Europe or the Middle East.

- I feel content when I've read a new book each month to expand my knowledge.

- I try to get enough exercise by forcing myself to be active at least three times a week.

- I must spend time with my immediate and extended families at least once a week.

Now take some time to prepare a list of the things that you believe are important to your success. How will your list compare to mine? What will you add? What will you change? Are there any points that you will delete? Label this List 1, and keep it to use in Chapter 3.

Why is defining success so important?

There's a joke about a client who asks a Chartered Accountant "What does one plus one equal?" The accountant replies, "Whatever you want it to be." Although this is a joke that usually only accountants find funny, it holds some truth. Accounting is an art that requires some creativity—in some situations, two accountants could come up with different numbers and both are correct! Accounting is not always right or wrong, black or white—there are gray areas in which accountants use judgment, which may lead to different results.

Similarly, there are many gray areas in life, and in the meaning of success. The beauty of success is that it can be whatever you want it to be. You have the power to make it anything *you* want. You're in the driver's seat and you're in full control. But what is your definition of success? This is the million-dollar question, and you must answer it before you can advance any further towards your success. This is where many people

> *"Success is a state of mind. If you want success, start thinking of yourself as a success."*
> *– Dr. Joyce Brothers*

fail—they don't know what their true desires are and ultimately end up feeling unsuccessful.

What happens when you follow someone else's definition of success? Simple: you aren't happy, and you don't feel successful. One of my goals is to live and work in Europe. If that isn't something that you want, but you end up doing because you're following my definition of success, you probably won't be happy with your new life and, consequently, you won't feel successful.

I have come to realize that if we don't sit down to think about what success means to us, and if we don't define our own success, then it will be defined by our family, friends, society, or other influential forces in our lives. When this happens, we may not be truly motivated to achieve success because it's not really our own and has no true meaning to us. Don't get trapped in someone else's definition of success—once you're trapped, you'll most likely feel like a failure.

> *"Let us be thankful for the fools. But for them the rest of us could not succeed."*
> *- Mark Twain*

The next chapter provides a step-by-step guide for how to draw a roadmap to get you to your success destination. But before you get to that stage, there are two things you need to do—figure out what your Ultimate Success is, and what makes you truly happy in life. When you're clear on these two points, only then can you begin to follow your path to success.

Identify your Ultimate Success

It's very important for you to develop your unique definition of Ultimate Success—the biggest success of all. Ultimate Success is not something you can achieve in a few months or even a few years. It takes an entire lifetime to achieve. When you have arrived at your Ultimate Success, you have fulfilled the main purpose of your life, and have met your overall goal.

What is Ultimate Success?

Everything you do in life should help bring you closer to achieving your Ultimate Success. When you look at it that way, it becomes clear that each success throughout your life is a journey, not a destination. Each success moves you ahead on the *Success* board, bringing you ever closer to your final destination, Ultimate Success. That's why it's so important to decide what Ultimate Success means to you, and to keep your eyes on your roadmap. Without the map, you may end up going in the wrong direction and never arrive at your Ultimate Success destination.

A story from my own family may help to illustrate what Ultimate Success means to a person. When I was 22 years old I was in France visiting my grandparents for the Christmas holidays, as was our family tradition. As a young woman my grandmother had always wanted to become a nun, but obviously my grandfather had convinced her to marry him instead.

On this Christmas Eve, while the whole family was gathered around playing games and singing carols, I saw my grandfather lean over to my grandmother and say, "Look how beautiful our family is. Isn't all this better than being a nun?" It was a very touching moment, bringing tears to many eyes and a beautiful glowing smile to my grandmother's face. At the time, I didn't really understand the significance of what my grandfather had said to her. But now that I understand the meaning of Ultimate Success, it has become clearer.

At that moment, he must have felt fully satisfied with all his achievements in life, and with how proud he was of his wife, children, and grandchildren. I've also come to realize that it was probably the moment at which he felt he had achieved his Ultimate Success. He couldn't keep this great feeling to himself so he shared it with his wife. I'm so grateful that I was there to witness this great moment because I've learned much from my grandfather.

> *"The difference between a successful person and others is not a lack of strength, not a lack of knowledge, but rather in a lack of will."*
> *– Vincent T. Lombardi*

Sadly, he passed away a few months later. This is how powerful achieving your Ultimate Success is—it's like safely arriving at your final destination, winning your game of life, and snapping that final piece of Lego into place. It's the most fulfilling feeling you'll ever feel in life, a feeling of complete happiness, satisfaction, and inner peace about your life's journey. I believe that once you achieve your Ultimate Success, you will no longer fear death—you will have achieved all your successes, you will feel ready to die with no regrets.

What will Ultimate Success be for you?

My grandfather's story is about him achieving his Ultimate Success. But how does a person know what Ultimate Success is for them? I've given a lot of thought to this, and I've found that the best way for me to define my Ultimate Success is to envision myself on my deathbed. I know that many people don't like to think about death, but this is necessary in order to define your Ultimate Success.

I start by imagining what it would be like if my doctor told me I had only two more days to live. How would I feel? Would I regret things in life that I hadn't seen or done? Would I regret not being rich? Would I feel ready to die? I don't know about you, but I'm far from being ready to die. If my doctor gave me this news tomorrow, I would die with regret because I have not yet achieved my Ultimate Success.

I don't deny that I feel very successful about my life so far, but I'm not ready to let go of life just yet. There are still many things that I haven't done or experienced, one of them being fatherhood. I want to have children and experience the satisfaction of watching them grow into positive role models. I want to see them happily married, financially stable, with beautiful well-behaved children of their own. For me, once I have the comfort of knowing that my grandchildren are in good hands, my purpose on earth will have been fulfilled. This is my Ultimate Success ... which is very similar to my grandfather's.

Now it's your turn to identify all the components that will contribute to your Ultimate Success. Picture yourself on your deathbed. What are you thinking? How do you feel? What are your regrets? I'm guessing that most of your regrets would involve family and people you know.

Perhaps you've lost touch with someone special in your life, or you had too much pride to fight for someone or something you didn't realize was worth fighting for at the time. All regrets count because they all indicate aspects of your life that are important for you to include in your life goals.

Make a list of all the regrets you would have. Then meditate on your list to figure out which potential regret is the biggest and most important for you. Which one, once fulfilled, will make you feel like you've reached your ultimate satisfaction in life? Once

> *"Happiness is not by chance, but by choice."*
> *– Jim Rohn*

you are able to pinpoint your biggest and most important regret, that will most likely be your Ultimate Success. Then put the remaining items on this list in order, so your biggest is at the top and your smallest is at the bottom. Label this List 2, and keep it to use in Chapter 3.

Happiness and fun are important too!

There's more to life than achieving your Ultimate Success. Life is a journey that is meant to be enjoyed. If you aren't having fun along the way you probably won't reach your final destination because, somewhere along the road, you'll get bored and turn back.

To avoid this happening, you have to make your game of life, your quest for Ultimate Success, fun. Think of yourself on an around-the-world trip. Won't it be a shame if you don't stop at all the interesting sites to see what the world has to offer? The same holds true for your journey to success. Every day of your life is like a small section of your travel route. You should make many enjoyable stops along the way, even though these stops may not appear to bring you closer to your Ultimate Success. In fact, they will help you reach your Ultimate Success, because they will bring you much happiness. With happiness comes better health, which generally leads to longer life expectancy. Living longer gives you more time to fulfill all your successes, and the more success you achieve the happier you will be with the outcome of your life.

So, it's time to make List 3: What makes you happy as you travel down life's path? It's surprising the number of people who have never thought of this! As a starting point, look back at your List 2, your "deathbed regrets." Think about it: if you're on your deathbed and you have regrets, those regrets must be about things that you truly value, and things that you would have liked to do differently or more often. When you frame these ideas in a positive way (as things you would like to do rather than things you regret not doing), they become statements of your true desires.

Since fulfilling these true desires will contribute to you having a happy, successful life (assuming that one of your goals is to be happy), you should definitely include them in your roadmap to success. The ideal success roadmap includes a mixture of "true desire" goals and your "Ultimate Success" goal. Remember that balance is the key—you need some fun along the way, but don't get sidetracked by pursuing too many desires at the expense of reaching your Ultimate Success.

Be sure you want every item on your list

Take some time to consolidate your three lists into one Definition of My Success list. It's a good idea to translate the items in List 2, your anticipated deathbed regrets, into positive statements. For example, if you listed "didn't spend enough time playing tennis," translate that to "play tennis more often," or something similar. You may also want to merge two or more similar items into one, and making these changes may give you ideas for more list items.

> *"Success is getting what you want. Happiness is wanting what you get."*
> *– Dale Carnegie*

Every item on your consolidated Success list should be something that you truly desire. You won't feel motivated to achieve a goal that you don't truly desire, or, when you do achieve it, it won't bring you happiness. To find out if something is truly desirable to you, ask yourself "Why do I want it?"

One of my success factors was to make a million dollars by the age of 30. I went through a long, tough thought process before I added this to my Success list. I realized that I truly desired to make a million dollars by age 30 because I've never wanted to be one of those fathers who works long hours each day to provide for his family. Those fathers are missing out on a very important thing in life—spending time with their wives and watching their children grow up. So I figured that if I made a million dollars before I had kids, I wouldn't need to work so hard and long when I began a family of my own. With that kind of money, I would be able to afford to spend less time at work and more time at home. When I asked myself "Why do I want to make a million dollars by the age of 30?" my response was "Because I want to be able to afford spending time with my family," not because I wanted to be rich or buy myself nice stuff. Spending time with my family is part of my plan to achieving my Ultimate Success.

Test each desire

I don't add a new item to my Success list (or change an existing item) until I've put it through a test. I assess the goal using four criteria to see if reaching it will make me feel successful. If the goal meets all four criteria, then I know it's worth pursuing and I add it to my list.

The four criteria that each of my desires must meet are the following:

1. My desire has to make me happy in the short term or bring me closer to my Ultimate Success.

2. My desire has to be healthy.

3. My desire has to be morally and ethically correct.

4. My desire has to be reasonable—something I am able to achieve based on my abilities, talents and finances.

These criteria are straightforward and simple. If a given desire fails any of these four tests, then it may be a waste of my time and money to pursue it. A desire really serves no purpose if it doesn't bring me closer to my Ultimate Success or if doesn't make me feel happy.

When is the best time to define success for yourself?

If you feel that your career isn't going as planned, then you should do something about it. If you're not happy with the amount of time you're spending with your family and children, this is the time to react and make some necessary changes. If you don't feel fit and healthy, start exercising—if you don't find the time for exercise now, you'll be forced to make time for sickness later.

It's never too late to make changes in your life, so there's never a bad time to discover and be clear on your definition of success. I always try to be proactive and avoid procrastinating as much as I can—why wait to do things tomorrow when I'm able to do them today?

Life is short. Enjoy every moment!

My brother-in-law opened the bottom drawer of my sister's bureau and lifted out a tissue-wrapped package. "This," he said, "is not a slip. This is lingerie." He discarded the tissue and handed me the slip. It was exquisite; silk, handmade and trimmed with a cobweb of lace. The price tag with an astronomical figure on it was still attached.

"Jane bought this the first time we went to New York, at least 8 or 9 years ago. She never wore it. She was saving it for a special occasion. Well, I guess this is the occasion."

He took the slip from me and put it on the bed with the other clothes we were taking to the mortician. His hands lingered on the soft material for a moment, then he slammed the drawer shut and turned to me. "Don't ever save anything for a special occasion. Every day you're alive is a special occasion."

http://www.hoopsu.com/motivgift.html

In the movie *The Bucket List,* Jack Nicholson and Morgan Freeman waited until they found out they were going to die before doing all the things that would make them happy. Don't follow the movie and wait until it's too late. Make your success list now and start working on it early so you don't run out of time to achieve all your successes. Starting to work towards your success will make you a lot happier, which you'll realize very soon.

Success requires a Snapshot

Creating your Success list is not a one-time exercise. Always keep your list handy and read through it from time to time. Each time you think of something you want to add, go ahead and do so. And if circumstances in your life change, make changes to your list to keep it realistic and achievable.

Let me share with you the process that I go through at least once a year to assess and redefine my success. Basically, I use a set of questions to help me take a snapshot of where I am in my life at that point. This helps me to identify which aspects of my life I'm not happy with. Once I've identified these problem areas, I'm able to work out a plan for how to tackle them and stay on the right path towards my Ultimate Success.

> *"Happiness is an attitude. We either make ourselves miserable, or happy and strong. The amount of work is the same."*
> *– Francesca Reigler*

Because success should be a well-balanced package, I've built my questions to cover things that are most important to me and are necessary for me to feel successful. This gives me a complete overview of where I am in my life with respect to family, friends, health, career, education and money. Each time I feel like I'm taking the wrong direction in my life, I go through this exercise to find myself again. This helps me ensure that I take the correct routes on my map that will bring me to success and happiness.

Here are six of the categories of questions that I use for myself.

Snapshot Questionnaire

► ABOUT ME – How do I feel about myself?

1. Do I feel happy every day?

2. Am I happy with who I see in the mirror?

3. Do I enjoy how I spend my free time?

4. Am I excited about my vision of the future?

5. Do I feel that I'm getting the most out of my life?

6. Do I feel that I'm successful?

► MY FAMILY – How do I feel about my family?

1. Am I proud of my family (parents, siblings, spouse, children, etc.)?

2. Is my family proud of me?

3. Do I get along with all my family members?

4. How big a part does family play in my life?

5. Do I spend enough time with my family each week?

6. Am I there for my family when they need me?

7. Is my family there for me when I need them?

▶ MY FRIENDS – How do I feel about my friends?

1. Do I have enough friends?

2. Do I spend enough time hanging out with my friends?

3. Do I enjoy the company of all my friends?

4. Do my friends understand me?

5. Do I understand my friends?

6. Am I there for my friends when they need me?

7. Are my friends there for me when I need them?

▶ MY HEALTH – How healthy do I feel?

1. Do I feel that I'm in good physical shape?

2. Do I get sick often?

3. Do I eat well each day?

4. Do I get enough sleep each night?

5. Do I get enough exercise each week?

6. Is my weekly exercise program enjoyable?

▶ MY CAREER – How do I feel about my career?

1. Does my job make me happy?

2. Am I at my desired position and salary given my experience and age?

3. Do I get along with my clients, colleagues, employees, and bosses?

4. Am I working reasonable hours each week?

5. Am I motivated each morning to get out of bed for work?

6. Do I feel that I'm making enough money given the amount of time I spend working?

▶ MY MONEY – How do I feel about my wealth?

1. Do I make enough money to cover my basic living needs?

2. Am I satisfied with my annual income?

3. Do I save enough money each year for my retirement?

4. Am I making enough passive income (interest and other income from investments) each month?

5. Am I happy with what I'm spending my money on?

The other categories that I question myself about include love, religion, volunteering, education, laughter, and travel. When you create your own Snapshot questions, make sure they reflect the needs and desires that you identified in your Success list.

Tackle the negatives

Whenever you use the Snapshot list to assess where you are right now, pay particular attention to all your negative answers. For example, if I answered no to "Am I motivated each morning to get out of bed for work?" my next step is to figure out what the problem is. Why don't I feel motivated each morning? Is it because it's been a while since I've taken a vacation? Do I feel overworked? Is it that I no longer enjoy the type of work I do? Am I feeling sick or tired? Before you can go any further, you have to pinpoint why you gave a negative answer. Once you have figured out the cause of the problem, you'll be able to do whatever is necessary to change your answer to yes the next time you go through your Snapshot questionnaire.

A few years ago, I was working on a six-month contract with a team of about 30 consultants. My task was to review the work of each team member to make sure they had done what the client company wanted. The work was very fast paced and challenging. I was enjoying every second of it, and I woke up every morning excited and eager to begin a new day. Once the project was completed, most of the consultants were asked to leave, but my contract was renewed. I stuck around the company without much to do, and I started having a hard time waking up each morning. The motivation was no longer there and I wasn't sure why. I went back to the drawing board to take a Snapshot of my work situation so I could understand *why* I was feeling unmotivated. It took me about two days to figure out what the problem was.

> *"Develop success from failures. Discouragement and failure are two of the surest stepping stones to success."*
> *– Dale Carnegie*

I had lost my sense of purpose. I had been hired to complete a project, and I had achieved that. I felt very good about my contribution to the project, but once it was done I no longer had a clearly defined task or role every day. I had gone from running around all day with a million things on my plate to suddenly having not much to do. I was bored with the slower pace, and it felt like it took forever for each working day to end. That's what was affecting my motivation, making it harder for me to get out of bed each morning.

Once I pinpointed the root cause of my negative answer, I had two options. I could either ask the client for a busier, more challenging assignment, or I could move on to a new client. I chose to move on, and that decision solved my waking up problems.

Every time you take your Snapshot and evaluate all your negative responses, you have to come up with a solution that works for you. Keep in mind that this solution has to be reasonable and feasible.

Reminder: Don't forget about happiness!

Happiness is the biggest key to feeling successful. It's not money as most people believe and, regardless of what people believe and, regardless of what people tell you, money can't buy you true happiness. The biggest happiness comes from the quality of our relationships with others. Many people who have realized this have made career changes by moving from stressful, high-paying jobs to lower-key, home-based jobs. By doing this, they created some extra time that they can spend doing things that make them happy.

Ask parents what the happiest day of their life was and you'll most likely hear a story of the day their child was born. Birth is a God-given miracle. We celebrate birthdays year after year, and they never get boring because the miracle of birth has an everlasting effect. Our parents will never forget this day and will always celebrate it.

Please don't forget that neither money nor fame on their own bring happiness. They may bring momentary satisfaction and a short-term thrill, but the happiness you derive from them is short lived and easily lost. And keep in mind that you seldom hear of a person's happiest moment involving making money. Money and fame can be part of your success roadmap, but they shouldn't be the only factors.

> *"Success is not the key to happiness. Happiness is the key to success. If you love what you are doing, you will be successful."*
> *– Herman Cain*

Here are some fun facts about income and happiness:

- In a national Australian survey from 2002, it was found that high income earners actually feel less satisfied and prosperous than low income earners! Only 5 percent of the highest income earners (more than $100,000 per year) felt prosperous, and just 13 percent were totally satisfied with life generally.

- According to U.S. statistics, wealthy people are only slightly happier than average. Furthermore, studies show that people who value money highly tend to be less happy than those who place highest priority on love and relationships.

Once you have your Success list and you're sure that every item you have really will contribute to your

Ultimate Success, you're ready to move on by making good decisions in your life that will help you achieve the feeling of success. The next step is to prepare your Roadmap to Success.

Chapter 3

PREPARE YOUR ROADMAP TO SUCCESS

In this section you will learn:

✓   What a success roadmap is.

✓   Of the need to have many roadmaps on your lifetime voyage.

✓   How to test each success before adding it to your map.

In Chapter 2, you prepared your Success list, which includes all the things you want from life and the deathbed regrets that you want to avoid. Now you're ready for the next step, which is planning the concrete actions that will help you achieve your Ultimate Success.

What is a success roadmap?

Great! Now that you've defined your success and know what it takes to feel successful, it's time to plan the journey of your life.

Keep in mind that if you haven't defined your own success, you're probably following a roadmap that you inherited from somewhere or someone else in your life. The first roadmap I inherited came mainly from my older brother, John, when I was in university. Back then, I had no idea what I wanted to make out of my life. John suggested that I take the same route as him and become a chartered accountant. This is where my career path started and when the roadmap to achieve this goal was handed down to me.

> *"Know where you are headed, and you will stay on solid ground."*
> *– Proverbs 4:26*

A few years later, I hit a roadblock. John decided to leave the chartered accounting profession altogether. I was left alone with an incomplete roadmap that was not based on my own definition of success. Once I realized that John's map would not work for me, it was time for me to think for myself and come up with my own map.

But what is a roadmap? It's your step-by-step instruction booklet, similar to the kind that is included in a Lego kit. Its purpose is to ensure that you accomplish everything you set out to do in a planned and structured way. It's like a GPS that guides you from point A to point B. It will get you to where you need to be as quickly and accurately as possible, guiding you through each step of the way.

A success roadmap is comparable to a street roadmap. Let's say that I'm planning to drive across Europe, starting from Portugal and making my way to Greece. How could I accomplish this without a map? It might not be impossible, but it would be difficult to complete the journey without getting lost. So, to ensure that I don't waste time by getting lost, the best thing is for me to plan my routes beforehand with the help of a highway map and a map of each city that I'll pass through.

I find that planning a trip ahead is vital because it clarifies exactly where I want to go and how to get there. If I wait until I arrive in Europe before I start planning my trip, I could encounter many unexpected surprises, such as not having booked enough days to drive all the way, not having enough time to visit every landmark I want to see, taking a boring and dull route that doesn't offer much scenery, and not having enough money to do the whole trip.

A success roadmap works the same way as a driving roadmap. They both provide step-by-step guidance—one guides you on the road while the other guides you throughout your life. In order for each to work well, you need to know *where* you're going and *when* you want to get there. When correctly prepared, your success map becomes a guide for your life journey. I believe in having a success roadmap so strongly that I devote considerable time and attention to developing my maps.

My Ultimate Success map

Knowing that John's map would no longer work for me, I began drafting my own map based on my personal definition of success.

First, I started with the highest level map, in which I marked my Ultimate Success as my last stop. From there, I worked my way backwards.

I already knew that my Ultimate Success involved having grandchildren, so I knew I needed to include having my own kids as a destination on my roadmap. Continuing to work backwards, I knew I didn't want children without being married, so I added marriage to my roadmap.

I wanted to be financially independent before I got married, so I set a goal not to get married until I could buy a house without having a mortgage. To achieve that, I estimated I had to make at least $100,000 net (after taxes) each year. But even at that early stage, in my twenties, I knew it wouldn't be possible to make that much money as an employee. I figured that I'd make more money if I was my own boss, so I included "being my own boss" on my map. But what does it take for someone to be a good boss? I figured that I needed a good education along with some good work experience at

> *"Success depends upon previous preparation, and without such preparation there is sure to be failure."*
> *– Confucius*

a reputable accounting firm on my roadmap. That told me that I had to start with a good education, so school became the first important success point on my lifetime success map. Once I realized that getting a good education was the first major step on my road to Ultimate Success, I focused hard on my studies until I received my chartered accountancy designation.

The next task was to set goal dates for when I wanted to arrive at each destination on my map. I decided to build this roadmap using my age, but that's not the only approach you could use. Depending on the map, you could specify the year, date, day of the week, or even the hour when you wanted to arrive at each destination on your map.

My high level roadmap to success looked something like this.

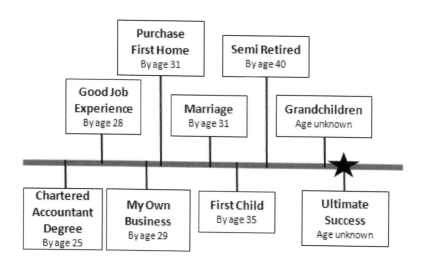

You need detailed maps too

Let's go back to our analogy about success maps being like roadmaps. Say I'm planning that driving trip across Europe. One of the first things I'll do is go to Google Maps to get a high level view of the route I'll need to take from Portugal to Greece. This is the map I get.

This overall map is great because it shows that I will be driving east (generally) through Portugal, Spain, France, Italy, and then Greece. Similarly, your high level success map shows the general direction in which you want your life to go, the major zones or periods that you'll go through along the way, and your final destination—your Ultimate Success.

But the Google map of Europe doesn't provide the details I need to make it successfully from Portugal to Greece without getting lost. It tells me the order in which I'll be driving through the countries, but I need to know exactly which routes to choose along the way. Similarly, your high level Ultimate Success map isn't detailed enough to provide you with the step-by-step instructions you need to follow to achieve your goals.

That's why Google Maps has a zoom feature. When I zoom in on the map of Europe, I get a much more detailed view. And the more I zoom in, the clearer the route becomes. I can see each street and each highway, which gives me the detailed instructions I need to guide me on my trip.

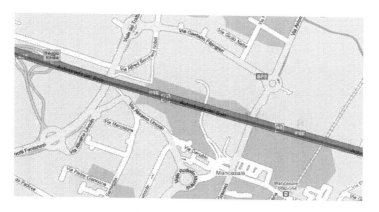

Your life map is comparable to the trip across Europe. Having your overall success roadmap isn't enough to achieve your Ultimate Success—you need more detailed maps that show you how to proceed through each stage along your route to your final destination.

How many maps will I need for the driving trip? Many! At a minimum, I'll need one map for each country I drive through. But I'd like to stop and visit some cities along the way, so I'll need maps of each of those cities in order to maneuver my way through.

The same applies to the map of your life. If you don't plan every step, every detail, then you risk feeling like a failure throughout your life. That's why it's necessary to zoom into your Ultimate Success map to get the details needed. Every big success should have its own map, and once you achieve a

> *"Arriving at one goal is the starting point to another."*
> *– John Dewey*

success, you continue living your life using the next map you have prepared. Each map connects to the one before it and the one after it, so that together they form a step-by-step path to your Ultimate Success.

I have prepared many maps to guide me through each day of my life. Each map is a "zoom in" on a section of my high level map. I started with a map for my education, which I successfully achieved in the year 2000. I put that map away and pulled out the next one—the map I had prepared for my career. This career map was built to take me on the long voyage over the next few decades of my working life. I'm still following my career map now, but it isn't the only one I'm following. I have other maps in my pocket—a financial map, a family map, a religion map, a friends map, and many other smaller maps. I haven't limited myself to just one map because one map wouldn't be sufficient for me to write down all the successes I want to achieve during my lifetime.

Using checklists with your detailed maps

Here is an example of my high level education map for my first semester at university.

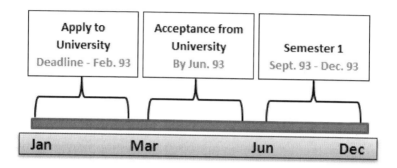

As you can see, it isn't very detailed, but this was just my starting point. From there, I zoomed in and continued to prepare a more detailed plan in a form of a checklist that looked like this:

Detailed Plan

A – Apply to University

- ❏ Apply for a Bachelor of Commerce degree with a major in accounting.

- ❏ Application deadline is end of February 1993.

- ❏ Application cost is $90.00, payable to the university by certified check or money order.

- ❏ Must include a copy of my high school diploma and grades.

B – Acceptance from University

❑ Acceptance expected to be received by June 1993. Follow up if not received by July.

❑ Apply for a student loan before the semester begins in September.

❑ Must attend the summer orientation session given in August.

❑ Must register for my first semester courses by August.

❑ Must purchase the books I need for my first semester before classes begin in September.

C – Semester 1

❑ Give priority to school and study at least 15 hours a week.

❑ Need a minimum grade of B– in all my accounting courses to go for a Chartered Accounting designation.

❑ Courses registered
- Introduction to Financial Accounting
- Introduction to Marketing
- Introduction to Microeconomics
- Introduction to Finance
- *(See class itinerary for more details of Assignments, papers, and exam dates)*

As you can see, my checklist gave me more detailed information about each success point that I had to achieve to make it through the first semester. But I didn't stop there. I zoomed in more to the point of planning my day-to-day goals. Here's an example of my calendar for a Monday and Tuesday during my first semester at university:

Daily Schedule			
Monday		Tuesday	
Time	Task	Time	Task
10:30 AM	Attend course: Introduction to Finance	11:15 AM	Microeconomics midterm
1:00 PM	Study for tomorrow's Microeconomics midterm	1:30 PM	Hang out at the mall with classmates
3:30 PM	Attend course: Introduction to Managerial Accounting	3:30 PM	Volunteering: After-school homework assistance program
7:00 PM	Kickboxing lesson	6:30 PM	Study
8:00 PM	Family dinner at home	9:30 PM	Go to a movie with friends

With this daily calendar, I knew where I had to be and at what time. It kept me organized and on track. Each task that I accomplished on time made me feel proud and successful because it assured me that I was right on track.

What you need to do

I can't tell you exactly how to draw your own roadmap, but I can tell you the thought process I used—and still use—to build my own maps.

As I discussed above, I began with my Ultimate Success and worked my way backwards to make sure I captured all my true desires and success points. I continued to categorize my success goals and desires into groups (such as family, school, work, entertainment, health, wealth, etc.), and then prepared a timeline for each group.

> *"All you need is the plan, the roadmap, and the courage to press on to your destination."*
> *– Earl Nightingale*

Draw timelines

You will begin by drawing a high level timeline for the items on your Success list (that you developed in Chapter 2). Mark "today" at the beginning of this timeline, and "end of life" (whatever age or year you intend to live to!) at the end. Divide the timeline into sections, using decades, years, or ages as the increments.

Now look at your Success list, and think about the date or age when you want to achieve this goal. For example, if one of your Success items is "live in Mexico for a year," do you want to do that in your forties? If one of your goals is to buy a house, when do you want to do that? Continue through your list, noting down the target date for achieving each of your successes. Then place each goal from your Success list onto the timeline in the correct place.

This timeline will be the basis of your planning for years to come, so think about the placement of your successes very carefully. Realistically, you probably can't put all of your target dates near the beginning of the timeline because some things take longer to achieve than others. Keep in mind that it may not be possible to achieve some successes before you have achieved others—for example, you need children before you can have grandchildren! It's also important to think about your priorities. Which successes are you the most anxious to achieve quickly, and which can you leave until later? Which successes will have to wait until you have more money in the bank?

There's no right or wrong order for the achievement dates on your timeline. The important thing is that your dates be realistic, and that you fit in every item from your Success list somewhere on the line. That way, you will achieve your Ultimate Success before you reach the end of the timeline.

Now that you have your high level timeline, you can create separate, more detailed timelines for each area of your life. For example, if your education timeline ends at "get a university degree," you need to write along the timeline the sub-successes that will get you to that larger success.

Gather information about each success

Begin by gathering all the information you need about each success to be able to map all the sub-successes on the timeline correctly. I do this by asking myself five questions about each success, to make sure I fully understand what it will take to achieve each success, and by when I need to achieve it.

> *"Every person, all the events of your life are there because you have drawn them there. What you choose to do with them is up to you."*
> *– Richard Bach*

Here are the questions I ask for each success.

1. Where do I want to go?

This is the success point I desire to achieve, whether it's my Ultimate Success or a true desire. When I'm at this point of my success mapping, I shouldn't be asking myself why I want to achieve that particular success, because I've already gone through that process (see Chapter 2). This question is really just to remind me of what my success goal is.

2. When must I be there?

I'm on the way to a movie that starts at 8 pm but I don't arrive until 11 pm. Yes, I have arrived at the right destination, but I'm too late. I can't call this success because I've missed the show! I have to know when I need to arrive at my destination to be successful. If I would like to lose five pounds by Valentine's day, then Valentine's day is the deadline for when I must be there. If I lose the weight by then, I'm successful. In general, answer this question with an age, a year, a date, a day of the week, or even a specific time during a day.

3. What do I need to take with me?

Before I begin a route, I need to do some planning to make sure I have everything I need before I hit the road. If I was looking for a job in the medical field, I'd need to make sure that I have a medical license before venturing down that route. Find out everything you need to have with you to achieve your success, and make sure you include achieving these things as sub-successes along your detailed timeline. If you wait until you reach the success door but you're refused entry because you forgot to bring something with you, it would be very frustrating and disappointing. So plan in advance for what you need along the way to achieving the success.

4. What do I do if I've hit a roadblock?

Life throws twists and turns at everyone, and you and I are not exceptions. The important thing to believe and remember is that a new door opens for every door that shuts in your face. In university, I needed to get a minimum grade of B– in all my courses to be eligible to apply for the chartered accounting program after I graduated. Well, in one course I got a disappointing grade of D+. That grade was definitely a roadblock—it was a threat to me becoming a chartered accountant. But I didn't give up. I adjusted my map to include taking the course over during a summer session. That time, I got an A– grade.

Keep in mind that there's no such thing as a simple route. Never consider giving up and turning back an option. Instead, make changes to your route to ensure that you navigate around the roadblocks you encounter and find another way to make it to your success point. In fact, thinking in advance about what roadblocks you might hit will allow you to come up with a plan B early, just in case you need it.

5. I've arrived—now what?

Congratulations on arriving! Unless you've reached your Ultimate Success, your lifetime route does not end here. You still have other successes to achieve, so it's time to pull out the next map that will bring you to your next success. When I was promoted to a level 2 senior auditor while working at PricewaterhouseCoopers, I knew that I had arrived at my desired success point. I had gained the work experience I needed to open my own accounting firm. Arriving to this goal made me move on to my next success, as outlined in my high level map, of becoming my own boss. Know what follows each of your successes so that you know what to tackle next.

Now that you know these five key questions, let me give you an example of how I've used them in the past. As you know, I wanted to be my own boss to take my career to a new level. So, obviously, this became a success point on my roadmap. But before I could figure out where to put this success in my map, I went through my five questions and responded as follows:

Where do I want to go?

This was pretty simple to answer because I knew I had to open my own business in order to be my own boss. Therefore my success destination was "my own business."

When must I be there?

I wanted to open my own business before I got married. According to my own high level roadmap, I had marriage circled in somewhere around age 30 to 32. Therefore, I had to aim to become my own boss before my 30th birthday. Now I had my timeframe for achieving this success.

What do I need to take with me?

The key to a successful business involves having good work experience, having good communication skills, and being a good networker. So, I worked on these things to make sure I had them all before I started my own business. That's why I waited until I got promoted before leaving my job at the accounting firm—my promotion was proof that I had obtained the necessary experience to be able to operate on my own.

What do I do if I hit a roadblock?

My response to this one was to keep thinking positively and continue working towards my goal. I told myself not to get discouraged, and to keep pushing forward because failure is not an option. If I didn't get the promotion at the firm in time to meet the deadline I had set for myself, then I was ready to work there for an extra year to get it. I was ready for that roadblock, but thankfully it didn't get in my way.

I've arrived—now what?

Once I became my own boss, it was time for me to move forward and look to my next goal—making the kind of money I had planned for in my financial roadmap. Starting my own business was also a step toward getting married and buying my first house.

It's your turn—start your engine!

Now it's your turn to start building your maps. I hope that you have found my tips and the accounts of my experiences useful. I know it can be confusing and difficult to draw a map, especially if it's your first one. But don't give up and don't get frustrated. These feelings are all normal and, over time, your maps will get clearer and make more sense. I've been building success maps for many years now

> *"A good plan is like a roadmap: it shows the final destination and usually the best way to get there."*
> *– H. Stanley Judd*

and I'm always making changes to the way I map things. Through trial and error, I've learned that some situations call for a graph, while others need a timeline, calendar, or checklist. Learning how to build good maps will take a big part of your life, so don't expect to be perfect at it right away.

Remember to begin by building an Ultimate Success map and then zoom in to get the information you need for each success to be able to map it. As you zoom in, start preparing your detailed plans, graphs, or schedules for everything you include on your map. Don't limit yourself to just one map. Prepare as many as you need—you can have one for education, another for work, and others for family and friends, leisure activities, and so on.

I wish you the very best of luck.

Chapter 4

THINKING THAT SUPPORTS YOUR SUCCESS

In this section you will learn that:

✓ A positive attitude is necessary in achieving your success.

✓ Life is filled with solutions, not problems.

✓ Everything in life happens for a reason and it's always for the best.

✓ Everyone is different, but no one is better than anyone else.

✓ Religion has many benefits that go hand-in-hand with success.

✓ Blaming everyone but yourself is the secret to achieving failure.

Y ou've done a lot of thinking and planning to get to this stage. Now it's time for me to share the tricks and secrets that support me as I'm traveling on my route to success. Over the years, I have observed that most successful people use these approaches. So I'm sure they will help you achieve success too.

Let's begin by talking about how the way you think can help you achieve your successes and your Ultimate Success.

Accept that you have to make it happen yourself

One of the biggest obstacles to success for some of us is that we always seem to be waiting around for our big break. We envision this break as a large sum of money, some great opportunity to get rich quickly, or simply a great job with an amazing salary. But what exactly are we waiting for? What are we expecting to get? From whom are we expecting to get it? And, even more importantly, *why* do we think we'll get such a break?

> *"Don't go around saying the world owes you a living. The world owes you nothing. It was here first."*
> *– Mark Twain*

Many people seem to think that opportunity means a chance to get money and happiness without earning it. I think most of these ideas come from movies, television, and the news media. On TV, people are making money easily through game shows and reality shows. The media are constantly running stories about people becoming instant millionaires by winning lotteries or through investing in the Internet or in real estate. Everyone seems to be making money but you! You start feeling angry towards your friends, your family, the government, and your job. You feel ripped off—that should have been you in the paper, winning the big lottery! You keep telling yourself that your break is just around the corner and any day now you'll be rich. And when you finally get that break, you'll be able to start living and do everything that you've dreamed about in life.

If you think this way, it's almost guaranteed that you will end up waiting and waiting. Before you know it, you'll be getting old and starting to realize that the break you've waited for your whole life will never come. Reality kicks in. Regret kicks in. You'll regret everything that you've missed out on in life—having the sports car that you've always wanted, going on that trip to Europe with your friends, and so on. You'll realize that at this point, dreams will always remain dreams. The disappointment and bitterness will make you grumpy and give you a sour outlook on life. Then all you'll have to look forward to is having a peaceful and painless death. Time is no longer on your side and your journey is over.

Take it from me—no one is going to give you a break. You have to make your own success happen. The only help in life that you'll get is from yourself. You and only you can take the necessary steps to achieve your dreams and your success.

Think of a few dreams that you've had over the past while and list all the things that you've done in the last year to achieve them. If I was to guess, I'd say that you've probably done nothing! Sitting around and waiting for your dreams to happen is neither proactive nor realistic. The odds of someone coming up to you with an opportunity of a lifetime are very slim, so don't waste your time and mental energy hoping for it. The only person who owes you anything is you—you owe it to yourself to make your success happen.

Stay positive

Your attitude plays an important part in determining whether you achieve your success or not. It's the first and most important secret to anyone's success. One of my university teachers stressed the importance of one's attitude. He always said that if we achieved a high grade in his course, it did not necessarily mean that we would find a well-paying job and be successful in life. He shared with us his formula for success—80 percent attitude and 20 percent intelligence. At the time, this didn't make sense to me, but my experiences since then have led me to agree with him completely.

What exactly is attitude? According to the Merriam-Webster dictionary, attitude is "a mental position with regard to a fact or state; a feeling or emotion toward a fact or state." Basically, it's the way you feel and react towards things that occur in your day-to-day life. Generally, your attitude can be either positive or negative. Your attitude makes the difference between feeling good about something and feeling bad about it.

The most important thing to realize is that you control your attitude. If your attitude is negative, it's because you have *decided* that it will be negative, and not because of other people or your circumstances. Having a positive outlook can mean the difference between succeeding and not succeeding, and between being happy and being unhappy. Your goal is to ensure that you always have a positive attitude towards everything that life throws your way.

A few years ago, I was returning home from a business trip in Charlotte, North Carolina, on a Friday. The connecting plane that I was to board in Philadelphia didn't have the software needed to fly to Montreal. For two hours the pilots tried to install the Montreal map in the system, but for some reason it wouldn't install properly. The flight was cancelled, and my fellow passengers and I had to spend the night in Philadelphia.

> "A man can get discouraged many times but he is not a failure until he begins to blame somebody else and stops trying."
> – *John Burroughs*

We were over a hundred people on that flight, and many people became angry and frustrated. To be honest, I felt some anger and frustration too—it had been a rough week, and I was looking forward to seeing my wife and having a relaxing weekend.

But before all my negative feelings started to pour out, I focused on the pros instead of cons and managed to keep a positive attitude towards the situation. I thought, I'd rather have the flight cancelled and spend the night safe and sound in a hotel in Philadelphia instead of testing out this newly installed software. God forbid, if the software causes an error in mid-air, the plane might crash! I'm anxious to get home, but I'm better off not being on that plane. I'll be home tomorrow—a delay of one day isn't a big deal.

But most people on that flight didn't have a positive attitude. Many lost their cool and yelled at the airline personnel. They didn't seem to realize that yelling and screaming wouldn't change the situation or resolve it. They also didn't realize that the people handing out our hotel vouchers had nothing to do with the decision to cancel the flight. These employees were simply doing their jobs. Why should they be yelled at and treated badly when they had nothing to do with the cancellation? Clearly, most of these passengers had a negative attitude.

But what difference did it make that a few of us had a positive attitude and the rest had a negative one? The positive people made the best of the situation. We were not angry, so we didn't stress out about it all night. We went to bed in peace and quiet, and got a good night's sleep. In contrast, the people with a negative attitude stressed over the delay all night long, complaining to one another and probably not getting much sleep as a result. They must have spent most of the night tossing and turning, only to wake up still feeling annoyed and frustrated.

This is where you need to work on yourself. Once you realize that your attitude is your choice and that you alone can decide how you deal with these kinds of events in your life, you'll be able to work on your reactions and feelings to make them more positive.

I've learned to find the positive in all situations that I encounter, which makes it easier to deal with most issues. If I only focused on the bad, everything around me would seem negative and harder to deal with. My attitude is that my perception becomes my reality. I control my attitude and my beliefs. If I believe something to be true, I can make it reality. To me, there's no such thing as failure—only results. My results are not always what I would like them to be, but at least I know that I can always work on my attitude and change my actions to produce more satisfying results.

> *"No one is a failure until they blame somebody else."*
> *– Charles 'Tremendous' Jones*

A positive outlook can mean the difference between succeeding and not succeeding, being happy and being unhappy. You must believe in yourself before others can believe in you. Push away all the negativity, because if you believe that your life is defined by narrow limits, you'll make those limits real.

Once you're able to find and keep a positive attitude about all the events in your life, obstacles that you encounter on your path to success will not be such a big deal. It's your attitude at the beginning of a task more than anything else that will determine your success or failure. With your positive attitude as your weapon, you'll simply conquer all obstacles and continue moving forward towards your success.

There are no problems, only solutions

I'd like to share a story about a man I met in Mexico. A bunch of us, all guys, went to Acapulco in the summer of 2007 for a bachelor party in honor of my older brother. We rented a big villa on the beach, which also had a private pool. We each had a suite, and the villa came with full service. We had housekeeping, two chefs, a gardener, security guards, a waiter, and a driver who stayed with us 24 hours a day during our five-day stay. For these few days, we were living like kings.

Arthuro, our driver, was in his early forties. He came with us everywhere, not just to drive us around, but to hang out with us and spend the day. He helped us bargain the best deals while shopping and he set us up as VIPs at all of the clubs we attended at night. Each time we had a problem, we ran right to him and he'd take care of it. He ate with us, drank with us and partied with us. He became part of our group.

Apart from Arthuro's outgoing nature and pleasant personality, what really stood out about him was his positive attitude. Every time we said, "Arthuro, we have a problem," he was very quick to respond, "No problems, only solutions!" We heard him say this over and over, and his saying became a theme of our trip. Every time we encountered a problem, we'd all sing in a joking way, "No problems, only solutions!"

We also started to behave differently when we encountered problems. Arthuro was like Superman—he had the ability to resolve anything. We were quick to drop "we have a problem" when we had to approach him with an issue. We had full confidence in him and, based on what he had been able to do for us, we knew that he could resolve any problem we had. So instead of telling him we had a problem, we started to say, "Arthuro, we need a solution." We adopted his style of positive thinking, changing our negative words and sentences into positive ones.

> *"If we can really understand the problem, the answer will come out of it, because the answer is not separate from the problem."*
> *– Jiddu Krishnamurti*

This is a change that we can all make in our day-to-day lives. When we start using positive words, it changes our attitude and our perspective on things. "No problems, only solutions" is something that I now use all the time. I feel that I can solve anything; I'm my own Superman!

When I encountered a problem before I met Arthuro, my brain gave me a signal that I might not be able to solve it, and sometimes I found myself at a dead end. But now that I've changed this thinking to be more positive—"no problems, only solutions"—the issues that I encounter have been transformed into fun challenges. Rather than getting nervous and anxious about a "problem," I feel excited because I enjoy fun challenges—responding to them is like playing a game. By just changing the way I think about challenges, I got rid of the problems that stressed me out and replaced them with enjoyable challenges.

Once I adopted this positive thinking, I felt that I could no longer fail. Nothing seemed to be that bad anymore. More and more I found that "problems" were just obstacles that needed a bit more of my attention. My mind was now thinking differently, and my attitude had become more positive. And it's all thanks to a wise man, Arthuro, who taught me that there's a solution to everything in life!

This is a great attitude to adopt in your day-to-day life. Life is full of solutions, not problems. The more you put this into practice in your life, the more faith you'll have in this approach. You'll start to truly believe that resolving issues and facing challenges are enjoyable, and your brain will change the way it sends signals to you. You'll find yourself more at ease each time you reach a roadblock on your route to success.

Making the attitude shift from seeing "problems" to seeing opportunities was an important part of putting me on the road to my success and keeping me there. Making this shift will work for you, too, I'm sure.

Everything happens for the best

To me, this is one of the most important attitudes that I have towards life. I truly believe that everything in life happens for the best, even though in most cases we don't see it that way at the time. The realization that bad experiences and events in our lives were actually good experiences in disguise often comes later in our lives.

> *"You know, sometimes bad things happen and you don't understand why and you just have to trust that there's a good reason for it."*
> *– Lois from television sitcom Malcolm in the Middle*

A few summers ago, my apartment was broken into. I had just started working for a new client in downtown Montreal. The contract was great, but the traffic getting there was so heavy that I moved temporarily into an apartment that was less than five minutes away from my client's office.

One Friday evening my friends and I had tickets to a soccer game that started at 6 pm, so I left my client a bit early. On the way there, I stopped at my apartment to change my clothes and meet my sister-in-law. Together, we then took the subway to the soccer stadium. Sandra, my fiancée (now my wife), couldn't leave work early so she was to meet us at the stadium a little after 6 pm. To our surprise, we bumped into Sandra at the subway station; she was coming out of the same subway car as we were about to go in. As soon as I saw her, I grabbed her by the hand and pulled her back in with us. She was surprised to see us because she thought that we would be at the stadium already. We then learned that she had managed to leave work early and was on her way to my apartment to drop off a few things that she didn't want to carry around.

The soccer game was fun, and filled with lots of action. When it was over, we all returned to my apartment to decide what to do next. While we were standing outside my door, I saw that the lock was lying on the ground. My apartment had been broken into, and they took everything! Gone were my wallet containing all my credit cards, my laptops, my external hard drives that held all my backups of client data, a cell phone, a $700 pen I got from Sandra as an engagement gift, cash, the blank signed checks, my clothes and, believe it or not, my toothbrush and deodorant.

But it didn't end there. A few weeks later, on the way home from a vacation, I found out that one of the thieves had gone to my bank pretending to be me, and had wiped out my bank accounts and line of credit. I thought, how much more of this can I take? My life was falling apart in front of my eyes and I had absolutely no control. I felt helpless. I couldn't return to my apartment because I felt so violated. I packed up all my remaining things and went back home, far from my client. And the bad news kept coming. I received a bill from an electronics store for $9,000. I was having problems with my clients because I had lost a lot of electronic files and had to redo at least six weeks' worth of work.

> *"Things turn out best for the people who make the best of the way things turn out."*
> *– Art Linkletter*

How could I possibly have a positive attitude about this? If "everything happens for the best," what could be "the best" in this situation? At first, I was in complete disbelief that I had lost so much in such a short period of time. I kept trying to figure out why such a thing would happen. How could a guy like me find himself in a position like this? Do all the good deeds I do mean nothing to God?

I kept thinking about it because I had to justify it. I had lost everything! How could this be for the best when I couldn't imagine anything being worse? And then, it finally clicked. How could I not have seen it earlier? Why was I so concentrated on what I had lost, instead of really focusing on what I had gained? I finally understood why God had let it happen and what God had prevented. What I had gained was worth a lot more than everything I could possibly own. Once I realized this, I was very thankful. I felt like I had won a million dollars.

At this point you're probably thinking that I'm crazy! But let me explain. Given that I had not taken a subway in years, what were the odds of my fiancée and me being at the *same door* of the *same train* at the *same subway station* at the *same time* this one time I took the subway? Was this fate? If the timing had been off by just two seconds, I wouldn't have seen her, and wouldn't have grabbed her and brought her into the car with me. If we had missed each other, what would have happened? I played this scenario over and over in my head. Whoever robbed me must have kept an eye on me. They must have broken in right after my sister-in-law and I left the apartment. If I hadn't bumped into Sandra at the station, she would have arrived at my apartment about 20 minutes after we left it. The burglar(s) would have already been cleaning out the place. What if Sandra had walked in on the burglars? Caught and in a panic, who knows what they would have done to get to the door. They could have beaten her, or tied her up, and it could even have gone as far as murder. But none of that happened because I bumped into her and pulled her into the subway with me where she was safe.

Once I got perspective on what had happened, I realized that God had kept Sandra safe at the expense of my belongings. And which situation do you think I would prefer—keeping all my belongings but Sandra injured by the burglars, or losing my stuff and Sandra safe? Like most people, I would choose option two without much thought. No price can be placed on a loved one.

We need to realize that in many instances, there's something (life, faith, God, angels—whichever one you believe in) keeping an eye out on us and helping to guide us in the correct direction when we need it most. Here's an inspirational story that I received in an email. I've tried to find out who the author is, but have been unsuccessful.

Things Aren't Always What They Seem

Two traveling angels stopped to spend the night in the home of a wealthy family. The family was rude and refused to let the angels stay in the mansion's guest room. Instead the angels were given a small space in the cold basement. As the angels made their bed on the hard floor, the older angel saw a hole in the wall and repaired it.

When the younger angel asked "Why have you repaired the hole in the wall?" the older angel replied, "Things aren't always what they seem."

The next night the pair came to rest at the house of a very poor, but hospitable, farmer and his wife. The poor farmer and his wife shared what little food they had with the angels, and let them sleep in their bed where they could have a good night's rest. When the sun came up the next morning the angels found the farmer and his wife in tears. Their only cow, whose milk had been their sole source of income, lay dead in the field.

The younger angel was infuriated and asked the older angel, "How could you have let this happen? The first family had everything, yet you helped him! The second had little but was willing to share everything, and yet, you let the cow die!"

"Things aren't always what they seem," the older angel replied. "When we stayed in the basement of the mansion, I noticed there was gold stored in that hole in the wall. Since the owner was so obsessed with greed and unwilling to share his good fortune, I sealed the wall so he wouldn't find it. Then last night as we slept in the farmer's bed, the angel of death came for his wife. I gave him the cow instead. Things aren't always what they seem."

http://godslittleacre.net/spiritualgrowth/things_arent_always_what_they_seem.html

This story demonstrates well that everything in life happens for a reason and it's always for the best! Not all things in life turn out the way we expect them to. Just have faith and trust that every outcome in life is always to your advantage, whether you know it or not. And sometimes you'll never know it. The farmer in the story will never know how close he came to losing his wife, but if given the opportunity to pick between losing his wife or the cow, I'm pretty sure he would have picked to lose the cow.

Once you learn to apply this attitude to your daily life, you'll start to notice that your perspective on life changes. You'll be more forgiving and happier with the outcomes of things, whether they appear to be good or bad. What used to

> *"Attitude is a little thing that makes a big difference."*
> *– Winston Churchill*

annoy you will now seem less important, and you'll start to realize that things could be worse.

One last story.

I used to work with a man who lost his pinky finger on this right hand. After his accident he was absent from the office for a few days and upon his return, all he did was complain about his loss. After two days of his complaining, I told him that it wasn't that bad and it could have been worse. "How can it be worse? I have lost a finger!" he responded a bit agitated.

This guy was letting the loss of his finger affect his attitude on life. He was feeling miserable and was full of hatred; he hated himself, hated everyone around him, and hated his life at that point in time. I was surprised how badly he was taking it because in my mind, I still believed that things could have been worse.

So when he asked me to justify how it could have been worse, my response was "It could have been your thumb." My response didn't make any sense to him because he raised his voice when he replied back saying "Who cares which finger it is. A finger is a finger and at this point, it would have been the same if they were all gone!" In an attempt not to make things worse, I stayed quiet and took a deep breath thinking of how I could get through to him without making a scene at the office.

I was thinking how wrong his attitude was. First, I'm pretty sure that he really didn't mean what he said about not making a difference if all his fingers were gone. There's not one person that would pick to have all their fingers lost when only one can be gone. And second, YES there's a positive thing about having lost a pinky finger: it's not his thumb!

Think about this...the thumb is the most important finger on your hand. Without it your hand becomes almost useless. As an experiment, try tucking your thumb into your palm and see if you can function for a few hours without it. If you're having trouble keeping your thumb tucked into your palms, try using Scotch tape or an elastic band to keep it tied down. You'll see that it's very difficult performing your day to day activities without the thumb. Try writing your name with a pen, or try to drink water from a glass (good luck holding onto your glass). It will only take you a few seconds to realize how important your thumb is, and how important of a role it plays as part of your hand.

Now perform the same experiment with your pinky. Hold it, or tie it down and try writing your name with a pen. You probably have no problem there. Drinking from a glass? Again, it can be done, not a problem. Yes, I'm sure you feel some discomfort having your pinky tied down but, guess what, your hand is more functional than when you had your thumb tied down.

So what's my point? It could have been worse for my colleague if he had lost his thumb. Instead of focusing on what he had lost, he should have focused on what he had gained. He could have lost the use of his hand but, instead, he managed to keep its functionality but lost the use of his pinky.

It wasn't until a few days later that I was able to explain this point to him. Once he realized that it could have been worse, his attitude changed. He did continue to complain from time to time about it, but at least the complaints were now followed with "thank god it wasn't my thumb."

The road to success is filled with many roadblocks and doors closing in your face, but once you've mastered the "everything happens for the best" attitude, you'll start to realize that for every door that closes, another opens. Even though it doesn't seem that way at times, one day it will be apparent to you. At the very least, when you encounter a roadblock you'll be able to think that whatever happened, it could have been worse—you could have been hurt. And if you were hurt, at least you did not die.

> *"God makes everything happen at the right time. Yet none of us ever fully understand all he has done."*
> *– Ecclesiastes 3:11*

You are not better than anyone

Sadly, the mistreatment of people is very common in our society. Many people have the attitude that they are "better" than others, because they tend to judge others based on income, ethnic background, education, religion, appearance, and many other factors. Rich people believe they are better than poor people, while white-collar workers see themselves as more valuable than blue-collar workers. But it doesn't stop there—the educated look down on the uneducated, Muslims pity Christians, and so on.

This all gets confusing because if *he* is better than *she*, and *she* is better than *they*, while *they* are better than *he*, who really is the better person? None of them—everyone is different, but no one is better than anyone else.

A Jewish friend of mine, Joshua, was one of my study partners in university. One day, my car was at the mechanic's so he offered to have his father drive me home after school. We walked over to his father's office, and his father had no problem giving me a lift. His father was actually a very outgoing guy, talking and asking me a lot of questions. He seemed genuinely interested in who I was and what

> *"If you judge people, you have no time to love them."*
> – *Mother Teresa*

my family did. Everything was great in the car on the way home until he asked, "What's your original nationality, Pat?"

I'm originally a Christian Palestinian, so I wasn't sure what to tell him because I know there's a lot of friction between the Palestinian and Jewish people. I figured that since his son and I had no problems with our differences, then the father shouldn't have a problem with it either. I told him the truth, that I was originally Palestinian, and from that moment he went silent and did not speak to me for the rest of the ride. Although he did not say anything bad to me, his silence was enough to let me know that he didn't like me. I had done absolutely nothing to this man, and yet I was immediately judged based on my original nationality. Trust me, the silent treatment I received from that man didn't feel good, nor was it justified. From that moment on, I've tried to treat people the same way I would like them to treat me. After all, we are all brothers and sisters, so why shouldn't we treat each other with love, respect, and politeness?

As humans, we are *all* built the same way. Whether rich or poor, we all need to eat and drink, we all laugh, and we all cry—If you cut me, I'll bleed, and if I cut you, you'll bleed too. We all have emotions and we all feel the need to be loved. So if we all have the same needs, how can any of us be better than the others? We're not!

My mother always stressed the importance of family and how she would never let me live on my own until I got married or had to move because of work. This way of thinking became part of my values and beliefs; I would also like to see my children stay at home until marriage. But I don't share this value with everyone. I once had a nurse come over to my house to perform a few tests and she believed the complete opposite. She told me that she made it a point to see that her son and daughter left the house as teenagers. Even though she found it very hard to let them go, she believed it was something she had to do to make her children stronger and more independent.

Am I better than the nurse for thinking that I need to provide for my children longer than her? No, my beliefs and values are just different. Better or worse is just a matter of opinion.

When I compare my life to that of my Little Brother's (from the Big Brothers program), I realize his life is surrounded by poverty, drugs, alcohol and theft, whereas my lifestyle is the opposite—I work hard, consume alcohol socially, live well and avoid illegal substances and activities. But does this make me a better person than him? Is my life more valuable? The answers to these questions are subjective—they're just personal opinion. I chose to live my life the way I believe is best for me, while his mother surely tries to do the same by teaching him and raising him the best way she knows how. We don't share beliefs, values, religious views, or life paths. But just

> *"You know something? As long as we've been here we've believed that, as aliens, we were superior. But what I've realized is that nobody is superior; they're all just different, that's all."*
> **– Dick Solomon** *from television sitcom 3rd Rock from the Sun*

because our lives are completely opposing to each other, I don't believe that my life is worth more than his, nor do I believe that I'm better than he is.

If I was to ask you "does a strawberry taste better than a pear?" your answer would be your own personal opinion, which is the point that I'm trying to make. Personally, I find that a pear tastes better, but if you ask my wife, she'll tell you she prefers the strawberry. The fact that I prefer the pear does not mean that it's superior to the strawberry because my taste preference is not shared by everyone.

Jesus leaves us with a parable on this matter. He told this story to some who had great confidence in their own righteousness and scorned everyone else.

Parable of the Pharisee and Tax Collector

"Two men went to the Temple to pray. One was a Pharisee, and the other was a despised tax collector. The Pharisee stood by himself and prayed this prayer: 'I thank you, God, that I am not a sinner like everyone else.

For I don't cheat, I don't sin, and I don't commit adultery. I'm certainly not like that tax collector! I fast twice a week, and I give you a tenth of my income.'

> The tax collector stood at a distance and dared not even lift his eyes to heaven as he prayed. Instead, he beat his chest in sorrow, saying, 'O God, be merciful to me, for I am a sinner.'"
>
> Jesus continues to say "I tell you, this sinner, not the Pharisee, returned home justified before God. For those who exalt themselves will be humbled, and those who humble themselves will be exalted."
>
> *Luke 18:10-14*

At the beginning of this book, I said that I wanted to be better than average. When I say this, I don't imply that average is bad, or that I see myself as better than the average person. I use *better* in this context to mean that I wanted to perform *above average*. There are many people who make an average salary and lead an average life, and they are very content with themselves. There's nothing wrong with being average but, in my case, I have always had a personal desire to be different. So in

> *"Love others as much as you love yourself."*
> *– Jesus*

order for me to achieve this difference, I base many things I do on the average, and then take a step or two further to go above and beyond the average. My need for this difference is what has driven me to achieve my success in each step of my life. Although I have always wanted to be different than the average person, I want to make it clear that I don't believe that I'm *better* than anyone else.

Assume everyone is important

A few years ago, I was standing outside a store when I heard someone shouting. I looked around and noticed a small crowd watching a woman who was standing outside a car window yelling at the driver inside. Before I had enough time to really understand what was going on, the woman's hand got caught in the car window as it started driving off. I watched the woman's body tumble onto the ground as the car turned the corner. I'll never forget the loud cries I heard from the woman as she lay there on the pavement. I made a mad dash towards her to help her up. Luckily, she did not have any serious injuries, just some minor cuts and bruises from the asphalt. I tried to comfort her, and offered to drive her home. There wasn't much more that I could have done, but at least I did something.

After dropping her off, I realized that no one, absolutely no one, else from the crowd had made an attempt to help her, which really saddened me. How could everyone just stand by and watch? Do we not care for others anymore? To this day, I'm puzzled by the insensitivity we show one another.

We don't always stop and think about others. We are selfish by nature, and usually put ourselves first. But we have to change this way of thinking. Life is precious and we have to realize that we are all the same, each one of us—we are all human. The woman I helped that day turned out to be a client of my mother's, and she had recognized me. The following day she called my mother to thank me for what I had done, and to invite us over for dinner. To this day, she remains a very faithful client of my mother's and thanks me each time I see her for my good deed. What she does not know is that I had no idea who she was and how important a client she was to my mother when I went to her aid.

The lesson I learned was to assume that *everyone* is important regardless of religion, race, sex, education, income or nationality. I try and treat people equally with the respect everyone deserves because I never know who I'm dealing with. I believe that you should treat everyone the same way that you would like to be treated. So if you like it when people open the door for you, make it a point to open the door for them, too. If they need help, help them. You have to respect everyone equally, regardless of their differences, because you really never know who you're dealing with. The next person you open the door for could end up being a key person who helps you on your route to success.

> *"He who gives to the poor will never be in need."*
> – *Proverbs 28:27*

I don't come first

Remember, I'm not better than you, nor are you better than me, so why should I treat myself better if we are equally important? Generally I don't treat myself better, nor do I put myself ahead of people around me. I feel that for me to be happy, I need to make sure that the people surrounding me are happy. And for me to achieve this, I can't put myself ahead of everyone. Instead, I have to become the servant and bow down to their needs.

Before I got married, I used to work a lot of overtime and frequently picked up food to eat on the way home. I sometimes encountered a homeless person on the way back to my car, so I'd give that person my food. My options were simple—either I ate, or the homeless person ate. Since I don't generally put myself ahead of anyone, the other person usually got to eat instead of me. Under those circumstances, it didn't matter when I went to bed hungry because I felt good knowing that my unselfishness resulted in someone else going to bed without a growling stomach.

I once worked for a client where it was customary to celebrate each employee's birthday with a cake. The client was always kind enough to invite me, and the other consultants, to these small celebrations. On a few occasions, there wasn't enough cake for everyone, so I always made it a point to be at the back of the cake line. I knew I wouldn't feel comfortable, or good about myself, grabbing a piece at the expense of another person.

This is the behavior that society is missing. We need to treat one another as equals without being selfish and without putting ourselves ahead of them. We have to help one another and extend our family to include friends, neighbors, colleagues and strangers.

The homeless are special too

Our society gets a major failing grade for the way homeless people are treated. Unfortunately, many of us have absolutely no respect for the homeless and curse their existence. We think that we are better than them because we work and they don't, or because we're clean and they're not. But the reality is that their needs are pretty much the same as yours—they need food, shelter, love and human contact on a daily basis, too. These are things most of us try to deny them

> *"Don't judge others and God won't judge you. Don't be hard on others and God won't be hard on you. Forgive others and God will forgive you."*
> *– Luke 6:37*

continuously throughout each day of their lives because we have categorized them as "bums." They are already faced with many difficult challenges, but instead of trying to help them out our society makes it harder for them.

Please don't forget that every person in the world, whether rich or poor, black or white, is human and has feelings just like you. How would you feel if everyone around you looked down on you and called you names? It doesn't feel good and trust me, each homeless person we see on the streets knows what society thinks of them. Our behavior simply adds to their problems.

A small exercise

Here's what you need to do:

- ► With a smile, go up to a homeless person on the streets and ask him how his day is going.

- ► Then, reach into your pocket and give him a $20 bill. The reaction you'll get from this will make you feel good, but please don't stop here.

- ► Next, give him a wrapped sandwich, a bottle of juice, and a bag of chips.

Now get ready to experience the best feeling in the world worth a lot more than the $30 value you just gave away. When I perform this exercise, the reactions I get are amazing. I've had my hand shaken, seen tears, been thanked 20 times nonstop, and I've even been hugged. All of which feel great. It's something you should experience yourself because once you've experience this feeling, you're going to want to feel it over and over again (and it's also good news for the homeless).

If you still believe you're better than others

Remember, feeling or believing that you're better than others is a matter of opinion, not a fact. If you truly believe that you're better than someone else, don't tell them. There's no value in letting that person know you believe you're better. After all, it's just your opinion. And putting other people down reflects negatively on you.

Constantly telling people that their way is wrong is a great way to create enemies. You can judge people in any way you want, but don't forget that there's always someone out there more successful than you, stronger than you, more popular than you, richer than you, better looking than you, or smarter than you. Rubbing something in someone's face will only make you look bad and encourages someone else to turn around and rub something in your face. Just keep your opinions to yourself and no one will feel the need to bother you when they themselves feel they are better than you at something.

Importance of religion

I was born into a religious Catholic family. My family tree shows four nuns and one priest just three generations away—One of the nuns, Blessed Mother Marie-Alphosine, is destined to be the first Saint from the Holy Land. With religion in my family blood, I was raised to believe in God and throughout my life, God has played an

> *"Everything you ask for in prayer will be yours, if you only have faith."*
> *– Mark 11:24*

important role in making me feel successful. Because of God's involvement in my success, I believe that religious faith can and should be an important part of anyone's success. But I don't just mean Catholicism—it doesn't matter which religion you live by, as long as your beliefs involve a God. The three largest religions in the world, Christianity, Islam and Hinduism, are all grounded in the belief that there is a God—a superior being who watches over us and judges us at the end of our lives.

Sadly, today's society is forgetting about God, and many people are abandoning religion all together. If we continue to allow this to happen, we need to understand how this lack of faith will affect our lives and the lives of our children. Religion offers so many advantages that it would be careless to just push it aside.

Why do we need religion in our lives? What good is it to us? These are questions I hear often, and they should be addressed. First, we have to give credit to religion as the bedrock of the idea of ethics. Imagine how life would be if the concept of ethics didn't exist in our society. I'd never be able to live in such a world. Religion tells us to be good people, to love our enemies, to take time to reflect on the goodness in the world, and to help those in need. Religious faith makes us better people and gives our lives greater meaning and purpose.

The benefits of religion

Let's look at some findings based on research studies:

 Regular attendance at religious services is linked to good health, stable family life, strong marriages and well-behaved children.

The practice of religion is also linked to lower rates of divorce, domestic abuse, other crimes, substance abuse, addiction, and suicide and depression.

 Religious people live more active, healthier and happier lives compared to their non-religious counterparts.

 Religious people tend to have more education, better work habits, and higher levels of self-control and self-esteem.

 Parents who are religious are more likely to enjoy a better relationship with their children, and are more likely to be involved with their children's education.

 There is a reduced risk of colitis, different types of cancer, and ultimately death among people with higher levels of religious commitment.

 Religion is also associated with higher recovery rates from addictions to alcohol and drugs.

 Very religious women have the greatest level of sexual satisfaction with their husbands!

As you can see, the benefits derived from being religious can include greater happiness, a longer life, and living in peace with the people around you. Each of these benefits has the potential to make you feel that your life is more successful, so the power of religion should not be underestimated.

It all begins with believing in God

Suppose you're at work, and your desk is on the same floor as your boss's office, the President of the company. You and your colleagues are all working hard to impress the boss in hopes of getting a promotion and a nice bonus at the end of the year. Now imagine what your work day would be like if the President was away on a business trip. His absence would probably change things. I imagine that you'd feel more laid back knowing that your boss wasn't there to monitor your every move. I'm sure the day's productivity would most likely drop as you take longer breaks for lunch and to chit-chat with your co-workers. After all, it wouldn't matter because the President wouldn't know about it. You're pretty much at liberty to do anything you want without getting caught.

> *"The more we depend on God the more dependable we find He is."*
> *- Cliff Richard*

This is how I view life when people don't believe in God. The boss is never around so people feel that they can do anything they want, whether good or bad. But because I have religious faith, God is my ultimate boss. He never leaves my side and *He* is the one who judges me at the end of my time. So I have to impress God by behaving and acting responsibly, not the President. With God's eyes on me 24/7, I'm strongly motivated to be a better person. I know that I can't fool God or hide anything from Him, so I have to think twice before doing something that I believe is wrong. I don't claim that I'm perfect, but I have no doubt that my life would be very different if religion didn't play such an important part in it.

God is with us always

Many time I've heard people ask "Where was God when I was going through my divorce?" or "If God exists, how can He let terrible things happen?" We must remember that everything happens for a reason, and to our best advantage. God has mapped everything out so that we get what's best for us at the end. Even during the difficult moments in life when we believe that God has abandoned us, He is still there helping us out—we just don't know about it. If you feel that God has turned His back on you at some point in your life, I want you to reflect on the story below, because it's important to understand the true and inspiring message it delivers.

Footprints in the Sand

Last night I had a dream that I was walking along the beach with the Lord. Across the sky flashed scenes from my life. For each scene, I noticed two sets of footprints in the sand: one belonged to me, the other to the Lord. After the last scene of my life flashed before me, I looked back at the footprints in the sand. I noticed

---

that at many times along the path of my life, especially at the very lowest and saddest times, there was only one set of footprints.

This really troubled me, so I asked the Lord about it. "Lord, you said that once I decided to follow you, you'd walk with me all the way. But I noticed that during the saddest and most troublesome times of my life, there was only one set of footprints. Why would you leave me when I needed you the most?"

The Lord replied, "My son, my precious child, I love you and I would never leave you. During your times of suffering, when you could see only one set of footprints, it was then that I carried you."

http://www.naute.com/inspiration/footprints.phtml

Rediscover religion

Do the best you can knowing that God's eyes are always on you. If you believe you're being watched all the time, you'll work a bit harder and treat people better. Religion provides structure and gives us the guidance we need to live peacefully. Religion opens our eyes, ears, and mind. It allows us

"Without God, man neither knows which way to go, nor even understands who he is."
- Pope Benedict XVI

to see God when we look for Him, to hear Him when we listen, and to understand Him when he speaks to us.

No matter what your religion is, I urge you to rediscover God if you have disconnected from him. Learn how to pray so that you can reach out to Him at any time. With God by your side, you'll surely start to realize how successful and happy you feel about your life. Each morning when you wake up, thank God that He has let you live to see a new day, and each night thank Him again for allowing you to make it through the day safely. Every day is a blessing for which we should all be thankful.

Don't play the blame game

The secret to achieving failure is blaming everyone but yourself. Since you want to achieve the opposite, you have to avoid the blame game! If you feel that you don't have enough money, it's not your employer's fault for underpaying you, or a friend's fault for not asking you to be part of his successful business plan, or your banker's fault for not investing your money in the most successful

> "*Even though the blame's on you, I will take that blame from you.*"
> – *Akon*

mutual funds, or the government's fault for taxing you too much. It's your fault. If you have always wanted to travel to Hawaii but haven't been able to, it's nobody else's fault. You should never point your finger to blame someone else for not achieving your successes for you.

My mother always told me that each time I blame someone and point my index finger at them, three other fingers are pointing back at me—in other words, it's actually more my fault than theirs. Only as I got older and wiser did I truly understand what she meant. Her point was simple: don't blame others!

In the Alcoholics Anonymous program, the first critical step to becoming sober is admitting that you're an alcoholic. Similarly, the first critical step to finding the road to your success is to accept that you are responsible for achieving your own success. Stop blaming the people around you for your  unhappiness. From now on, you have to realize that you're in full control of yourself, your life, your happiness, and your success. Remember, life owes you nothing—you owe it to yourself!

Chapter 5

ACTIONS THAT SUPPORT YOUR SUCCESS

In this section you will learn that:

✓   Your inner voice is important in discovering the secret to your success.

✓   Visualizing your success is important in making it become your reality.

✓   Volunteering builds teamwork and provides valuable professional development opportunities.

✓   Exercise gives you the strength and power you need on your path to success.

✓   If you lived your life like a dog, you would achieve success overnight.

I n Chapter 4, we discussed the secret of using the way you think to support your journey to success. But thinking positively and staying in the right frame of mind no matter what isn't enough in itself. You must also "walk the talk"—be proactive about doing things that will bring you closer to achieving your success. That's what this chapter is all about.

Listen to your inner voice

We all have a voice in our head that tries to speak to us from time to time. We have all experienced a situation in which we are about to do something but pause and think twice because a strong feeling—a voice in our head— warns us that something is wrong. We all hear the voice, but do we really listen to it? Most of us choose to ignore it by pushing it aside, thinking that listening to it may be a sign that we're crazy or foolish. But stop! Your inner voice is important in discovering the secret to your success.

Here's a scenario that I'm sure has happened to many of us. You're dieting, vowing not to eat anything sweet for a few weeks. Then, while visiting a friend, you're offered a dessert that makes your mouth water. What's the first thing that happens? Your inner voice tells you, "You shouldn't eat that, you're on a diet." When this has happened to you, how did you deal with it? Did you eat the dessert or not? If you turned the dessert down, pat yourself on the back for doing a good job at listened to your inner voice.

Who is your inner voice and why is it so important? Where is it coming from, and what does it have to do with success? These are easy questions to answer because that inner voice is simply *you*! The voice is your intuition and sense of morality—it's the insight and wisdom that comes from your subconscious mind. It knows everything about you, and it's like the tiny angel version of you that we often see in cartoons, sitting on our shoulder across from the devil. Your inner voice gives you warnings and tries to convince you to do the right thing when you encounter different situations in your everyday life.

Make a point of listening each time you notice your inner voice talking. Don't take it for granted because there's no one in the world who knows you more than your mini you does. Let it guide you through making the right decisions on your road to success, because it always points you towards moral and ethical solutions that you truly believe in. This may sound simple, but in reality it's not. Most of us often completely contradict what our inner voice tells us because we simply don't like what it's saying.

> *"There's a voice inside you that tells you what you should do."*
> *– Alan Rickman*

We start to argue with it by using logic and probabilities, and we keep arguing until we're sure the voice loses.

When I first left my well-paying job to start my own accounting firm, it wasn't easy to go from a good salary to nothing at all. I spent months with no income, trying to find my first client. I finally found a new business in desperate need of accounting advice and services. I met with the owner to discuss the company's needs, and during the meeting I went through my fee structure. All was going well until the client said that all his start-up costs had left him short of money, and that he could only pay me 35 percent of what I was requesting.

Initially, I heard my inner voice telling me, "Poor guy, it's hard starting up a business. Have sympathy. Money isn't everything." But within seconds my logic and greed kicked in and I remember thinking that this guy didn't see what a great deal I was offering him. My hourly charge rate by my previous employer was above $300, and here I was, offering this client a rate of $65 per hour, and he was saying it was too much. I attacked my voice, thinking, "How can I accept $20 an hour when I'm worth above $300 on the market? It doesn't make sense. How can he expect someone with my qualifications to work for such a small amount?" I was surprised by my client's request, and confused about why my inner voice was telling me to have sympathy for him.

I left the meeting feeling discouraged and insulted. But after thinking about it, I realized that my inner voice was correct. It knew what the correct decision was for me immediately, based on the fact that I value helping people in need more than I value money. I had momentarily forgotten this important value during my meeting because I was too focused on making this business deal according to my own terms. Luckily, I made the effort to listen to my inner voice and figure out why it was telling me to be sympathetic. I realized that my voice was right, and I accepted my first contract as an independent accounting consultant.

Earning money was an important achievement in itself, so my decision paid off immediately. Looking back, I also realize that it was the first step in the rapid success of my business. Through this client, I learned new things, made new business contacts, and had my first experience in dealing with the federal tax authorities. Had I ignored my inner voice based on my logical argument that my proposed fee was very reasonable, I would have missed out on many opportunities.

> *"Do not follow the ideas of others, but learn to listen to the voice within yourself. Your body and mind will become clear and you will realize the unity of all things."*
> *– Dogen*

Your inner voice is with you for life

Our inner voice starts speaking to us at a very young age. Children know that eating a cookie before dinner is wrong (because their inner voice tells them), but they usually ignore it. This is evident by the fact that they try to sneak a cookie from the jar when nobody is looking. Without their inner voice, they would take a cookie openly, because they wouldn't know right from wrong. The fact that they try to be sneaky about it demonstrates that they have an inner voice telling them it's wrong. However, they aren't mature enough to realize the significance of the voice, so they go against it.

As we grow older, we can't use the immaturity excuse anymore. We are now able to hear and understand the voice, and yet many of us still choose to fight against it. For example, I'm sure that married adults who have affairs constantly hear their inner voice talking to them. Actually, it's most likely screaming—we all know that cheating is against society's beliefs and morals, so their inner voices probably scream at them a lot.

So why do people still cheat when their inner voice is screaming? I believe that many people try to rationalize the situation by using excuses and logic to counteract their inner voice. "My wife is out of town, so she'll never find out"; "It's only this one time so it's okay"; "It was a mistake, I was drunk"; or "It's only sex, it doesn't mean anything to me." They only feel better about what they're doing when they have won the argument and silenced their inner voice.

This is simply a bad habit, and it's one that you can and should break. Each time you hear your inner voice, stop and listen to it. Try not to argue or push it aside. Remember, your inner voice is *you*! And only you know exactly what is best for you. Keep in mind that your inner voice is never wrong! What may be wrong is the way that we interpret what it's trying to say to us.With your mini you by your side, your journey to success will be smoother and easier.

Go ahead and close your eyes right now and just listen. What is your voice saying?

Use visualizations

When I was 23 years old and preparing for the Chartered Accountant exam, I had a dream one night in which I passed the exam. It was such a happy dream that it occupied my mind for days to follow, and I wished that I had never woken up. I wanted this dream to come true so badly that I found myself constantly daydreaming, repeating the dream over and over in my head. I even started adding extra things that were not part of my original dream. This is when I realized that my visualization was a form of acting—not in public, but in my head, where I was my only audience.

In my daydreams, I started to extend the visualization to the exam room. I saw myself sitting there writing and writing, using my calculator, leaning back to think. I had no idea what the exam room actually looked like, but I made one up and acted it out in my head.

I also thought about how I would react hearing the news that I had passed. My older brother John had written the same exam 3 years before me and I was there to experience his reaction when he passed. I had never seen him so happy and I too wanted to experience the same feeling of happiness. I kept wondering how I would react. Would I jump around happily like John, or would I break down and cry? Rather than waiting to get my exam result,

I started to act out my reaction in my head every day. I saw myself in front of the computer, stressed and nervous, with a drink by my side to calm my nerves. I pictured myself entering my user ID and password and waiting a few seconds for the results to pop up onscreen. The more I played this scene in my head, the more details I could see. Eventually I started to see the sweat building up on my forehead, and I could feel my heart pounding in my chest. The visualization started to affect my reality—I got goose bumps every time I got to the part where I found out that I passed, jumping around with extreme excitement. By this time, I had become an Oscar-winning actor, and it was all in my head.

How visualization works

How would you know what success is if you can't see it in your mind? That's why you have to mentally act it out for an audience of one—you! You have to force yourself to see it, to want it and finally to touch it. If you want to get into a room, first you knock on the door to see if someone will let you in. If you don't get an answer, you take matters into your own hands,

> "The most important thing is to pretend, as best you can, that something is true."
> – *Mark Fisher*

turn the knob and walk right in. You can't just sit by the door hoping that someone will eventually invite you in. Your success is right behind that door so you need to do whatever it takes to get in.

When you start to see something in your mind, your desire to have it becomes greater. When you visualize it, it starts to become reality. Your subconscious mind works with you to attain your goal. If you want something so much that you can taste it, your brain starts to push you in that direction. You'll find that the visions will occupy your mind more often, and the more you see them, the more you'll want them. And with your increased desire, you'll start working towards your goal, and won't stop until you've reached it—until you feel as good as the picture in your head. So the better you act out what you want in your head, the more of a reality it will start to appear to you.

You may not always achieve your goal the first time around, but don't worry about it. All you have to do is dust yourself off and try all over again. There's no limit to the number of times that you can try to achieve something that you want. What's important is that you never give up and keep trying until you finally get what you want. Keep in mind that if you never try, you'll never get what you want.

Dreaming yourself to success is a learned behavior— you have to practice. Make it part of your daily routine until you get better and better at it. But keep in mind that visualization alone will not bring you to your success. You also have to take action—that's what eventually transforms your daydreams into reality.

Once you have mastered the visualization technique, you can apply it to everything you do in life. I use it every day with everything I do. If I'm asked to prepare a report for someone, I play it all out in my head to the point where I can see exactly what the report looks like and how my client reacts when I give it to him. Once I visualize what I want and what my client expects, I start taking action to make the vision my reality.

Visualizing needs music

When I was discovering the power of visualizing, a song called "Graduation" was very popular. Whenever I heard it, I envisioned my own graduation after passing my Chartered Accounting exam. I saw my friends there, high-fiving each other, and I saw my family sharing the proud moment with me. That song was very special for me, and to this day I believe

> *"Success often comes to those who have the aptitude to see way down the road."*
> *– Laing Burns, Jr.*

it played an important role in helping me pass the exam on my first attempt.

At the same time, I picked another song to help me out when I was having difficulty preparing myself for the exam. When I scored poorly on an assignment or practice exam, I played Aaliyah's "Try Again." The chorus lifted my spirits whenever I heard it or sang it: "If at first you don't succeed, then dust yourself off and try again. You can dust yourself off and try again...."

Music plays a very important role in lifting up our spirits, so it's a good idea to incorporate it into your route to success. Now it's your turn to visualize. Remember, seeing is believing. If you can't see it, you can't achieve it.

So are you ready to act? I'm sure you are. 1 ... 2 ... 3 ... ACTION!

Volunteering leads to success

Most people who are successful are well-rounded—they think about the well-being of others as well as themselves. I once saw in a survey that 90 percent of executives in Fortune 500 companies believed volunteering builds teamwork and provides valuable professional development opportunities. Whether people volunteer in their community for an hour a week or devote much more time to their volunteer work, they experience the great benefits that volunteering brings to themselves, to other people, and to society as a whole.

"Until I started giving, I never really appreciated how much I have."
– Dick Solomon from television sitcom 3rd Rock from the Sun

Volunteering makes you a better person while you give back to society by helping those in need. This made me decide that I needed to have volunteering experience.

I've been volunteering since 1998, when I began helping immigrant children with their homework after school at a church. Since then, I've become a Big Brother, handed out food baskets and served meals at homeless shelters, volunteered during the Pope's visit to France, sold Christmas cards for an organization for the mentally challenged, handed out Christmas toys to underprivileged children, and a few other small commitments. The more I volunteered, the more I discovered that it was fun and very rewarding.

It's not always easy to find time for volunteering, but I make it a point to fit it into my schedule. People who say they don't have the time to volunteer really mean that they prefer not to make the time. Think about it—if I gave you concert tickets to see your favorite band next weekend, would you be able to make the time to go? Most people would. Where there's a will, there's a way.

Volunteering has added more meaning to my life because I'm not always fully satisfied by the work I do every day. Many charity organizations allow their volunteers to pick the work they want to do, so I choose things that I really enjoy doing.

Let's take a quick look at the top four benefits that volunteering will bring to you on your road to success.

Learn new skills

Some of the skills I have learned and improved through my volunteer work are patience, leadership, listening, public speaking, teaching, time management, prioritizing, and how to be a good team player. Many non-profit organizations have staff and volunteers from different backgrounds, ages, and ideologies. Working with them gives you the opportunity to see the many different ways there are to do things, and to see which approaches are the most effective in which situations. You can learn a lot by watching and listening to others. You can then experiment with these approaches yourself in a risk-free environment—since you aren't getting paid, you can't get fired as long as you don't damage the reputation of the organization.

My first volunteering experience in 1998 involved an after school program helping immigrant children with their homework. I was trying to teach one of the children fractions and she just could not understand the concept of it. Out of frustration, I accidentally broke my pencil in front of her into 3 pieces and used it as an attempt to help her understand. To my surprise, she did understand. I was surprised that she understood because I did not intentionally break the pencil, it just happened. Accidental or not, it worked and I figured that she needed to see the 3 different pieces to understand how you can divide 1 by 3.

> *"Happiness comes when we test our skills towards some meaningful purpose."*
> *– John Stossel*

That moment opened my eyes to a new world, a world of doing things differently. I had learned something new; it was my breakthrough. I discovered that I needed to teach the children in a visual manner by using objects as examples. From then on, all my teachings involved demonstrations with toys or drawings to help them visualize things. It made it easier for me to teach and they understood it quicker, which made their learning experience more enjoyable.

Using visual effects while teaching is a skill that I continuously use now in my career, whether in training courses or in meetings. I have also become good at training new employees since I'm very patient and use techniques which are simple and clear. Volunteering definitely has paid off for me.

A volunteering environment is a perfect setting where you can keep experimenting with different approaches until you finally find what works best for you.

Here are some relevant facts from surveys:

- More than three quarters (79%) of volunteers said that volunteering helped them with their interpersonal skills, such as understanding people better, motivating others, and dealing with difficult situations.

- Just over two thirds (68%) said that volunteering helped them develop better communication skills.

- Just under half (49%) of employed volunteers aged 15 to 24 said their volunteer activities gave them new skills that they could apply directly to their job.

  – 2000 National Survey of Giving, Volunteering and Participating.
  http://www.givingandvolunteering.ca

94% of employers believe that volunteering can add to skills.

94% of employees who volunteered to learn new skills benefited by getting their first job, improving their salary, or getting a promotion.

– World Volunteer Web

68% of employers feel that volunteering can add skills to their workforce.

43% of employers think that employees who do volunteer work and learn new skills have a better chance of promotion and earning a higher salary.

– Guardian News and Media Limited Guardian

Feel good about yourself

Volunteering gives you the satisfaction of knowing that you're making a difference while doing something you enjoy and believe in. You'll get words of praise and appreciation when you mention to friends and family the great activities you're involved in.

> *"The best way to cheer yourself is to try to cheer someone else up."*
> *– Mark Twain*

But I don't only feel good about myself because of the feedback that I get from other people. Much of it comes from the cause itself. I feel great as I watch my Little Brother (from the Big Brothers program) growing up, and we have a lot of fun together. When I was helping the immigrant children after school, I enjoyed being a part of their advancement in their education and lives. For me, the most rewarding feeling comes from helping the homeless. I've never felt such sincere appreciation and kindness.

As long as you're doing something that you truly believe in, your experience will make you feel like you're floating on a cloud. It's a priceless feeling knowing that you're making a difference to people and to a cause that you believe in.

Become a leader

In many cases, as a volunteer you'll have a lot of freedom to get things done the way you want to. You're given a goal, and it's up to you to decide how to achieve it. This forces you to be creative, which in turn develops your problem-solving and leadership skills. In effect, you act as your own boss, and in the process you learn how to be a leader.

Nobody taught me how to help the children with their homework; it was up to me to figure it out. I had to try different ways until I found the one that worked best for me and the kids. And since I was truly motivated to help them do better, I rose to the challenge.

Find new job opportunities

Employers are impressed by people who volunteer, because it shows that you're dependable, responsible, caring, and hard working. It also indicates strong commitment and time management skills. Volunteering makes your employer look good so make sure you list all your volunteer work on your resume.

Volunteering also offers great networking opportunities. You'll meet people from all parts of society who have a wide variety of paying jobs. Over the years, I've been asked by volunteer buddies to help them find a job, and I've signed up new clients. You never know who might be volunteering by your side—it could be a human resources manager for a company you'd like to work for, or someone who's the perfect candidate your company is looking for.

> *"Sometimes you can become rich by being generous, or poor by being greedy."*
> *– Proverbs 11:24*

The more involved you are in your volunteering, the more visibility you'll have. For example, a great way to increase your exposure is by participating in fundraising events. You'll meet a lot of people from the sponsoring companies. Take the opportunity to market yourself—talk to as many people as you can.

More relevant facts about the value of volunteering:

 Over half (55%) of volunteers aged 15 to 24 said that they volunteered to improve their job opportunities.

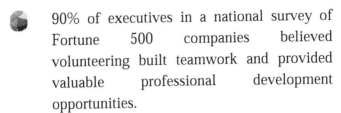 90% of executives in a national survey of Fortune 500 companies believed volunteering built teamwork and provided valuable professional development opportunities.

– *2000 National Survey of Giving, Volunteering and Participating.* http://www.givingandvolunteering.ca

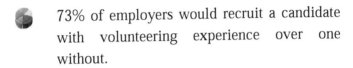 73% of employers would recruit a candidate with volunteering experience over one without.

– *World Volunteer Web*

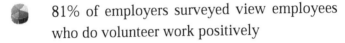 81% of employers surveyed view employees who do volunteer work positively

– *Guardian News and Media Limited Guardian*

Starfish

Once upon a time there was a wise man who went to the ocean to do his writing. He had a habit of walking on the beach before he began his work.

One day he was walking along the shore and as he looked down the beach, he saw a human figure moving like a dancer. He smiled to himself to think of someone who would dance to the day. So he began to walk faster to catch up.

As he got closer, he saw that it was a young man. The young man wasn't dancing—he was reaching down, picking something up, and very gently throwing it into the ocean.

As he got closer, the writer called out, "Good morning! What are you doing?" The young man paused, looked up and replied, "Throwing starfish in the ocean."

"I guess I should have asked, why are you throwing starfish in the ocean?"

"The sun is up, and the tide is going out. And if I don't throw them in they'll die."

"But, young man, don't you realize that there are miles and miles of beach, and starfish all along it. You can't possibly make a difference!"

The young man listened politely. Then he bent down, picked another starfish and threw it into the sea, past the breaking waves and said, "It made a difference for that one."

http://www.inspirationalfood.com/View/tabid/77/ArticleID/87/CB ModuleId/383/Default.aspx

Your volunteer work doesn't have to make a difference to the whole world—you just have to make a difference to at least one person. Everyone has needs and feelings, and as long as the people you're helping feel your generosity, you've already made a difference.

Now go out and make a difference!

Exercise, exercise and more exercise

I'm sure you have heard a million times how important it is to exercise regularly. Well, I'm here to tell you the same. Exercise is the key to a healthy lifestyle and is a great tool to make you feel great. This, in turn, gives you the strength and power you need on your path to success.

My parents always ensured that I led an active life. As long as the sun was out, I was outside with my brothers and friends being active. But as a teenager, my focus changed to driving around with friends, listening to music, and girls. My focus no longer involved sports and I was no longer interested in my bike and skateboard.

When I hit university, I did sports on the weekends, but my free time was limited so I was not able to be as active as I would have liked to. After university, as my work became more demanding, I worked more and exercised less. I started to feel the toll of this stress on my body, so I joined a kickboxing group. It didn't take many lessons for me to start to realize how good my body felt to be active again.

> *"Those who think they have no time for bodily exercise will sooner or later have to find time for illness."*
> *– Edward Stanley*

I felt my self-confidence starting to improve which made me feel good about myself. This improved my mood which made me a happier person. I was sleeping better and physically, I had more energy and felt stronger. Although my muscles were aching most of the time, the pain was a nice reminder that the kickboxing was having a positive effect on my body.

I had rediscovered the importance of exercise and I was reaping the benefits from it. But what are these benefits?

Let's look at the emotional benefits first. When you exercise, your body produces chemicals called endorphins. These endorphins make you feel happier and more relaxed—they improve your mood and lower your stress levels. Regular exercise also helps you fall asleep faster, and gives you a deeper sleep. This improves your mood, concentration and productivity. Make exercise a routine in your daily life and see how quickly you begin to feel better about yourself. Just make sure that your timing is right because it may end up backfiring on you if you exercise too close to bedtime. You get a boost of energy from exercising so you should give yourself about 5 hours before going to sleep to burn off all of the energy.

Of course, exercise also brings you physical benefits. It combats heart disease by managing your blood pressure, and lowers bad cholesterol while increasing good cholesterol. It also strengthens your back muscles, which in turn reduces back pain. Regular exercise can prevent diabetes, osteoporosis and certain types of cancers. Since exercise makes your heart and lungs work better, it gives you more energy to do more things each day of your life. You'll burn more calories, which helps you control your weight. And here's a bonus: exercise improves your sex life. So don't be selfish—if you don't want to get in shape for yourself, at least do it for your partner's sake!

When you put all the emotional and physical benefits of exercise together, the result is that you'll live a longer, happier, more productive life. And that will help you achieve and enjoy all your successes!

One of the biggest reasons people drop an exercise program is lack of interest. Exercising doesn't have to be a chore. There are hundreds of sports and activities for you to try to find out which ones you enjoy, so don't limit yourself to a gym or an exercise machine. Find something fun!

If you're short of time, make it a point to get as much exercise as you can while you're working. If you work in an office, don't get discouraged. Walk around as much as you can, and make a habit of going for a walk during your lunch break. And take the stairs instead of the elevator! Every step you take brings you one step closer to better health, so do as much as you can whenever you can. Your success depends on it.

"If your dog is fat, you're not getting enough exercise."
– Unknown

Avoid could have, should have, and would have

My wife wins the gold medal on this topic. She is always saying "you should have done this" or "you could have done it this way." She's usually right that if I had done things differently the outcome *would have* served me better. But I didn't and now it's too late; what's done is done. If I spend my time and energy worrying about how I should have or could have done things, then I'm stuck in negative thinking, which will never get me anywhere or solve anything.

Could have, should have, and would have are all scenarios of how things *could have* turned out but **did not**; they are fictional, not a reality.

As an accountant, I've seen and heard many clients make mistakes or unsatisfying business decisions. I had a client call me a few months after the personal tax filing season was over in a panic because she had just found out that she could have deducted automobile expenses on her tax returns. "I'm so stupid, I should have asked my accountant to deducted my automobile expenses on my tax returns last year" she said to me. "I didn't know that I could have included them until a friend mentioned it to me over lunch. If only I had known, I would have gotten an additional tax refund of $2,000!" I soon discovered that this error had haunted her for many months and she had been complaining about it to many people before she finally decided to try and get some closure by calling me. Instead of worrying about the past, I told her that it wasn't such a big deal and that it was time to move forward. On that note, I presented her with a few options of things she 'could' do to rectify this issue. "You could simply re-file your taxes to include the automobile deductions and I would be more than glad to help you out with it." She seemed very relieved by my proposal.

We all could have or should have done many things differently in the past, but worrying about it or stressing over it adds no value. Everything in life should take you forward, not freeze you in the past. When I realize that I *should have* done something differently, I learn from it and apply it to my future—I don't let my past mistakes drown or stall me. Mistakes are great

> *"To be upset over what you don't have is to waste what you do have."*
> *– Ken S. Keyes, Jr.*

lessons, and if you don't learn from your mistakes, then the lessons are lost. I use my regrets and mistakes as a tool to make me stronger as I move forward.

But don't banish *should, could* and *would* from your vocabulary completely! They're great words on their own, without *have* attached to them: "you should fix it like this," "you could just apologize," "you would need to lose five pounds." These are all positive comments that are a proactive way to solve problems.

So when you catch yourself using a negative sentence that includes "I should have," turn it into a positive to resolve the issue by saying "I could ...." Turn "I should have claimed my car expenses on my taxes last year" into

"I could re-file my tax return and ask for a reassessment." Turn "I should have apologized for being late" into "I could call the person right now and apologize."

Use your mistakes as learning opportunities, and take action to fix the past so you can move forward into the future. On your road to success, you'll encounter many obstacles and often find yourself in the should have, could have, and would have world. If you're not prepared to brush them off and move forward, you'll drown in your past and you won't be able to reach your successful destination.

We can all learn from dogs

I received an email from a friend that pretty much says everything I wanted to say about this subject, and a whole lot more. It's too bad I don't know who the author is because I would really like to give that person credit where it's due. Here it is.

Belker the Dog

Being a veterinarian, I had been called to examine a 10-year-old Irish wolfhound named Belker. The dog's owners, Ron, Lisa, and their little boy Shane, were all very attached to Belker, and they were hoping for a miracle. I examined Belker and found he was dying of cancer. I told the family we couldn't do anything for Belker, and offered to perform the euthanasia procedure

---

for the old dog in their home. As we made arrangements, Ron and Lisa told me they thought it would be good for 6-year-old Shane to observe the procedure. They felt Shane might learn something from the experience.

The next day, I felt the familiar catch in my throat as Belker's family surrounded him. Shane seemed so calm, petting the old dog for the last time, that I wondered if he understood what was going on. Within a few minutes, Belker slipped peacefully away.

The little boy seemed to accept Belker's transition without any difficulty or confusion. We sat together for awhile, wondering aloud about the sad fact that animal lives are shorter than human lives. Shane, who had been listening quietly, piped up, "I know why."

Startled, we all turned to him. What came out of his mouth next stunned me. I'd never heard a more comforting explanation. He said, "People are born so that they can learn how to live a good life—like loving everybody all the time and being nice, right? Well, dogs already know how to do that, so they don't have to stay as long."

http://www.petsincondos.org/WhyDogs.htm

Because life is so short and precious, we should live simply, love generously, care deeply and speak kindly.

Remember, if a dog was the teacher you would learn things like

- When loved ones come home, always run to greet them.
- Never pass up the opportunity to go for a joyride.
- Allow the experience of fresh air and the wind in your face to be pure ecstasy.
- Take naps.
- Stretch before rising.
- Run, romp, and play daily.
- Thrive on attention and let people touch you.
- Avoid biting when a simple growl will do.
- On warm days, stop to lie on your back on the grass.
- On hot days, drink lots of water and lie under a shady tree.
- When you're happy, dance around and wag your entire body.
- Delight in the simple joy of a long walk.
- Be loyal.

- Never pretend to be something you're not.

- If what you want lies buried, dig until you find it.

- When someone is having a bad day, be silent, sit close by, and nuzzle them gently.

- ENJOY EVERY MOMENT OF EVERY DAY!

I hope you enjoyed this email as much as I did because the message it teaches is fantastic—if we could all learn to live like a dog, we would achieve success overnight because our lives would be filled with lots of happiness, friendship and good health.

Chapter 6

MANAGING YOUR MONEY

In this section you will learn that:

✓   Having a budget should be part of your success map.

✓   Credit cards provide many benefits when used wisely.

✓   Smoking is a financial disaster.

✓   Saving and investing your money can get you things for free.

✓   Doing things yourself can save you money.

By now, you have realized that money alone is not a good measurement of success. You can buy a house, but not a home. You can buy a clock, but not time. You can buy a bed, but not sleep. You can buy a book, but not knowledge. You can buy a visit to a doctor, but not good health. You can buy position, but not respect. You can buy blood, but not life. You can buy sex, but not love. Therefore, your Ultimate Success shouldn't be based solely on money.

In our society today, the average person doesn't manage their household income successfully. Year after year, the statistics show that most people are falling further into debt. Did you know that the average American household debt is $117,000 and the average Canadian household debt is $96,000? I find these statistics frightening, because if people who have jobs still find themselves spending more money than they earn year after year, then there's an apparent money management problem.

> *"A banker is a fellow who lends you his umbrella when the sun is shining, but wants it back the minute it begins to rain."*
> *– Mark Twain*

I've discussed debt with many people in my life, and I've been told many times that there's nothing wrong with being in debt because *everyone* in our society is in debt. Carrying debt from one year to the next is considered normal. But I disagree. Debt is like a piranha that will munch on you bit by bit throughout your life until you're left with nothing. And it's dangerous to believe that debt is normal. If that's what you believe, then your body and mind will work subconsciously to push you deeper and deeper into debt.

The key to being good at managing your money is to understand money and not fear it. I've always been fascinated with money. When I was just 7 years old, I ran a "store" at home, trying to convince my parents, brothers, friends, and family members to buy the candy I had that I didn't like. As far back as I can remember, I have always tried to find ways to make a few bucks, and to this day it feels good to watch my net worth increase. Unlike the average person, my net worth is positive and continues to increase from year to year. I have accomplished this by following two very simple principles:

1. Never spend more than you make.

2. Always remember that no one else will help you keep or make money—all anyone cares about is finding ways to somehow transfer your money to them. So I'm careful with my money (but not cheap), and avoid spending carelessly.

Once you understand these principles, you have taken the first step towards successfully managing your money. The next step is to develop healthy money habits. The following are some habits that have helped me to increase my financial wealth.

Have a budget

In Chapter 3, I talked about how important it is to have roadmaps that will guide you to your success goals. Having a budget is part of my success map, and it should be part of yours too. Think of a budget as a financial roadmap—as such, it's an important part of your Ultimate Success map.

What happens if you don't have a budget? Let me explain using a friend of mine as an example. Dave was always saying how one day he would love to have a brand new BMW. When he got an unexpected bonus and pay increase at work, he ran out and leased a BMW, not thinking about how much it would cost him.

> *"A budget tells us what we can't afford, but it doesn't keep us from buying it."*
> *– William Feather*

He assumed that since he was making more money, he should be able to afford it.

Dave's excitement was short-lived. Within months, he realized that the balance in his bank account was getting smaller every month, and he was having a harder time paying his bills. Dave realized that his lease payments, gas, and car insurance cost more than he had expected. His dream BMW was putting him into a hole, and he started to regret his decision to get the car. Every time he drove the car, Dave was reminded of his poor decision. He started using his credit cards to help him pay his monthly car, home, and personal bills, which pushed him even deeper into debt.

Dave's experience shows what can happen to a person or family that doesn't have a clear, sound budget as part of their roadmap. If Dave had prepared a budget to figure out how the BMW would affect him financially *before* he signed the lease agreement, he would have realized that his bonus and pay increase wouldn't be enough for him to afford the car. He would then have been able to make a decision based on logic, rather than his emotions. Dave's failure to do this led him to violate the first principle— once he signed the lease, he began to spend more than he made.

Fortunately for me, I discovered the advantages of budgeting many years ago, and I frequently consult my budget on my road to financial success. My budget helps me control my spending and helps me to stay on track without overspending in certain areas of my life.

I balance my budget by making sure that I have at least 30 percent of my monthly income left over after I pay my bills. My rule is that I shouldn't spend more than 70 cents of every dollar I make. The remaining 30 cents is what I invest wisely to generate passive income. This passive income is what keeps my net worth continuously growing.

Before I buy something, I check my budget to see if I can afford it. If I spent blindly, without having an idea of how much I can afford, I would probably spend more money than I have. If I spent more than I have, I'd be breaking the first principle, which means that I'd be pushing myself into debt. And debt is something that I won't accept for myself.

Here are some simple steps each person should take in preparing a simple budget.

1. **INCOME** – Figure out how much money you make in a month. This is usually the easiest part

of preparing a budget because most people already know what their income is. Make sure to include everything you collect in a month—your salary, investment income, rental income, and so on.

2. **MONTHLY EXPENSES** – Write down all your expenses during a typical month. If you're preparing a family budget, write down all the expenses for the entire family. For this exercise to be effective, you have to track *everything* you, or your family, spend money on. Don't forget to include the little things bought each day, such as coffee, gum, and newspapers.

3. **NON-ROUTINE EXPENSES** – Write down the expenses that you (and your family, if applicable) incur from time to time. These could include buying gifts in December, taking an annual vacation, hosting a few barbecues in the summer, and so on. You need to capture all of your non-routine expenses in your budgeted expenses. Think long and hard to make sure you record all the non-routine expenses you may incur. Once you've identified them all and put a realistic dollar figure on them, divide the total value by 12 to give you a per-month amount.

4. **COMPARE** – Deduct your monthly expenses and the per-month amount for your non-routine

expenses from your monthly income. If the result is a negative amount, you're spending too much money in at least one area of your life, and this over-spending will gradually put you deeper and deeper into debt. You need to prepare a realistic budget for yourself. If the result is a positive amount, pat yourself on the back. But this doesn't take you off the hook—it would still be good to have a budget because you may discover that you could be saving a lot more money each month.

5. **PREPARE A BUDGET** – Now you're ready to create your budget. Here are the steps to follow:

(a) Make a list of your expense categories, including your monthly and non-routine expenses. This list becomes column 1 of your budget.

(b) In column 2, write down your budget amounts—how much you believe you *should* be paying for each item in the list. This budget amount will become your "ceiling" amount for that category every month—your goal is to keep your expenses either at or below that ceiling amount. Your current monthly expenses should give you a good starting point for deciding what you think are realistic ceiling amounts for each item. For further help in setting your budget amounts, you can always search online for what the average person (or family) pays monthly for each expense category and use that as your budget amount.

6. **ANALYZE** – Keep track of everything you spend, and at the end of each month record the amounts in column 3 of your budget. Then, in column 4, put the difference between your budget amount and your actual spending (Budget – Actual = Difference). If the number you record in column 4 is zero or more than zero, then you're on target because you haven't spent above your ceiling amount. But if the number in column 4 is less than zero for any items, then you have two choices— you can either change your budget amount for that type of expense or cut back on your spending in that area to keep in line with your budget.

> *"Some couples go over their budgets very carefully every month; others just go over them."*
> *– Sally Poplin*

I use a software package called Quicken to track all my income and expenses. I highly recommend Quicken as a great tool. The software costs about $50 to $75 and will benefit you for many years. If you are unable to include the purchase of Quicken in your budget, then you can always prepare a spreadsheet to track all your spending, or even keep track of everything on hard copy in a budget book.

Appendix 1 is a blank copy of the budget template that I use for myself. Using this as a guide, and following these step-by-step instructions, you'll be able to prepare a budget that suits your needs and lifestyle.

It's never too late to prepare a budget, or a few of them; I actually have many different budgets. Budgets can be done on a day-to-day basis, monthly, quarterly, or yearly. There's no right or wrong way to prepare one, as long as you have one that works well for you and helps you control your spending in an efficient and profitable way. Also, don't forget to make sure that you have money set aside for investing as part of your budgets each month because, as you'll read shortly, investments are a big key to managing your money efficiently.

Use credit cards wisely

I got my first credit card when I was 16. My mother got me the card under her account to teach me financial responsibility—she wanted me to learn about debt and bill payments from an early age. None of my friends had a credit card, and I thought I was very cool for having one. Everywhere I went I swiped without worrying about how I'd pay the bill. I thought I was getting credit for free, and I felt like I could afford anything I wanted. My credit limit was only about $300, so my minimum monthly payments weren't very high. I was always able to borrow the money from family or friends to make that minimum monthly payment. I loved my credit card so much that the second I turned 18, I applied for my own cards. By the time I was 22, I had four credit cards and each new card I got made me feel older and more mature. Until this point, all was going well.

But things changed during the last years of my university studies. I knew that my mother was struggling financially to fund my education, so I decided to pay for my studies myself. Each semester I applied for a government student loan, but every time I was refused. With no government assistance, I turned to my credit cards to pay for my courses and books. This was the beginning of my credit card troubles. For a full-time student

> *"The credit card industry is out of control, it's getting away with robbery."*
> *– Robert Heady*

without a full-time job, this was a serious problem, because it was difficult for me to pay the monthly minimum balances on each card. By the time I graduated, I had a massive credit card debt—approximately $10,000.

At the ridiculous credit card interest rates as high at 28 percent, I was being charged interest fees of more than $200 each month. When I reached a point where I couldn't pay my minimum balances, I started withdrawing money from one card to make the payment on another one. I was stuck in a vicious cycle that was dragging me further into debt every day. Those plastic cards that I once loved so much had become my worst enemies. I knew I was in trouble and I needed to do something fast.

Once I started my career, my top priority was to rid myself of my credit card debts. I drew up a special credit card roadmap to get myself out of this debt as quickly as possible. My roadmap had three actions in it.

First, because I was lucky enough to still be living at home, I didn't have expensive household bills to worry about. I calculated that I only needed half of my paycheck to cover my day-to-day expenses. The most important step in my roadmap was to use the other half of every paycheck to pay down my debt. When I deposited my paycheck into my bank account every two weeks, I immediately transferred 50 percent of it to pay my debts. I didn't wait for the monthly credit card statements to arrive, because I knew that interest charges are calculated daily. Making the payments every two weeks reduced the amount of interest I had to pay in the end, and it guaranteed that I wouldn't spend the money on something else.

Second, I decided to stop using my credit cards. I destroyed the three cards that had the highest balances to remove the temptation of using them, and kept one card with me for emergencies.

The third step in my roadmap was to use cash instead of the credit card. If I wanted to buy something, I checked the cash in my bank account to see if the money was available. If it was, I bought what I wanted. If the money wasn't available, then I had two options—wait a few weeks until I had enough money to buy it, or simply change my mind about wanting it.

I stuck to my roadmap with strict discipline, and the results were excellent. I got myself out of my *full* credit card debt in less than a year, and I learned how costly credit card debt can become. This experience made me wiser, and the moment I finally became debt free I promised myself that I'd try to never be in debt again.

I got into the habit of checking my credit card transactions online. I check my online statement every week, and once I'm satisfied that it's accurate, I pay off the balance in full. By doing so, I'm ensuring that I never make a late payment. Also, I find it easier to cope with small weekly payments than to wait until the monthly bill arrives and be faced with a much larger payment.

> *"You want 21% risk free? Pay off your credit cards."*
> *– Andrew Tobias*

Credit card danger signs

In today's society, it seems that everything is moving from cash to plastic very rapidly. You may think that it would be impossible to get by without a credit card, but it's becoming more and more expensive to have them. More people are finding themselves with credit card troubles every day, which cause much stress and worry and can damage a family financially and emotionally.

But there's some good news. If you learn to use credit cards wisely, they can bring you great benefits. But before you can begin to use the cards to your advantage, you need to be debt free and, more importantly, you need to know the danger signs that indicate you have credit card troubles.

You're in trouble with your credit cards if:

- ☹ You don't have cash in your bank account to buy something, but you buy it anyway using a credit card.

- ☹ You don't pay your balance in full every month.

- ☹ Your card is maxed out and you can't pay off the full balance.

- ☹ Your card is maxed out and you're only able to pay the minimum monthly amount.

- ☹ You're struggling to pay off your monthly minimum balance(s).

- ☹ You're unable to pay off your monthly minimum balance(s).

- ☹ You find yourself using one card to pay off another (as I did in university).

If you are experiencing any of these warning signs, you're most likely heading towards serious credit card troubles. When I was using one credit card to pay off another, I had pretty much hit rock bottom. For some time, I had managed to fool myself into thinking that I was paying off my debts this way. But in reality, I was just borrowing more money from the credit card companies.

Take a look at your credit card statements to see where you stand. If you have any debt, work out a roadmap to get out of it as soon as possible, because credit card debt is expensive!

Yes, there are benefits

Despite the above, I'm not against credit cards. You can get many benefits by using a credit card correctly, and these benefits can result in a lot of financial reward. What I'm against is paying hefty charges and staggering interest rates. That's why the first step to using credit cards wisely is to eliminate all debts on them. Only once all debt is paid off does it become beneficial to take advantage of the benefits credit cards offer.

The following is a list of the main reasons why using credit cards can be beneficial for you.

 Credit cards are the best way to build credit history, which is essential in today's world. Without a good credit history, it's more difficult to get loans, mortgages, insurance, and sometimes even a new job. When you do get a loan, your credit score is used to determine the interest rate that will be charged on the loan. If you have a poor credit score, you'll be charged a higher interest rate, which means your payments will be higher. To get a good credit rating, you have to use a credit card and pay your bills on time. In fact, paying off your balance every week, which is what I do, is a great way to establish good credit history.

I've saved a lot of money on interest charges over the years by avoiding them completely. Also, because of my great payment history, my interest rates have been lowered on my credit cards and line of credit, which saves me money over my lifespan. And with my above-average credit score, it's easier for me to get a loan anytime I need one, at a reduced interest rate.

> *"Social security, bank account, and credit card numbers aren't just data. In the wrong hands they can wipe out someone's life savings, wreck their credit and cause financial ruin."*
> *– Melissa Bean*

Get a copy of your credit report to find out what your current score is. To do this, go online and search for either TransUnion or Equifax. These companies charge a small fee for a copy of your credit report, along with your credit score, and they usually provide it to you instantly. Once you've obtained a copy, you'll know whether you need to take the necessary steps to improve your score and reap the benefits.

 Many credit cards offer rewards, such as cash back, airline miles, discounts, rebates, gift cards, and so on (keep in mind that the rewards offered vary from card to card). These rewards are designed to get people hooked into using their credit cards as often as possible. But if you avoid that temptation and continue to use your card wisely, these reward programs can earn you a lot of money and more spending power.

The key is to resist going on a spending spree just to buy things that will earn you more reward points. Continue to use your card only to buy things you need and only when you have the cash in your bank account to pay it off. With each swipe, your reward points add up, and it's amazing how quickly you'll see the benefits. In 2009 alone, I had racked up close to $3,000 in reward points. With these points, I was able to get lots of great stuff, from free vacations to electronics to cash back. On my card, the reward points are equivalent to money.

For me, the most exciting rewards are those related to travel. Apart from allowing you to hold reservations, many cards provide trip cancellation insurance, medical insurance, and collision insurance on a rented car.

Get to know what reward programs and insurance coverage your credit cards provide you. Once you know what each card is good for, use it wisely to maximize your benefits from it.

 Another benefit is that every transaction related to your credit card is logged, and you can view this log online at anytime. Most credit card companies also provide detailed transaction logs that you can download easily into programs such as Quicken and MS Money. Tracking all my finances on Quicken allows me to generate reports that show me exactly where my money is going, how much I'm spending, and how much I'm worth. This information is very useful when I'm going through my actual versus budget amounts each month.

Of course, if you used cash instead of a credit card you could still have a log, but you'd have to keep it yourself. You would have to remember to write down the type of expense and the amount you spend every time you open your wallet, which is very labor intensive. When you use a credit card, you simply download your transactions and everything is there for you.

 Every time I withdraw money from an ATM or use my bank card to make a cash payment, I'm charged two service fees. The first charge is from my bank, and the second is from the ATM company. Each time I write a check, the bank charges me a 75 cent fee. Knowing that I get charged transaction fees by my bank, I try not to use checks, ATMs or my bank card to purchase anything. I just use my credit card—each swipe is free! It's true that many credit cards come with annual fees, but these are much less than a whole year's worth of ATM fees. Not only that, but I'm benefiting from the free points reward programs. So when faced with different payment options, save yourself some bank fees by using your credit card.

Know how to use your credit cards and you can reap many benefits and cost savings from them. Just remember the most important points—charge only what you can afford to pay for, and pay the bills off in full each month. If you can discipline yourself to hold true to that, you'll save a lot of money over the course of your life by using credit cards wisely.

Stop smoking

I've always found that smoking is one of the worse decisions anyone can make in life. It's not enjoyable to smoke, it tastes bad, smells bad, and it's bad for the health. How could we justify spending our money on something that doesn't give us anything good in return? We can't!

In addition to the many negative effects smoking has on your health and the health of the people around you, smoking comes with a high financial cost.

In Canada, the cost of a pack of cigarettes can range from $7 to $12, while in the United States it ranges from $5 to $10. This may not sound like much, but some people smoke more than a pack a day. Over the long term, this is very costly.

Let's look at Stephanie, a hypothetical example. To make the calculations easier, let's say a pack of cigarettes costs $5. Stephanie buys and smokes a pack a day, so her annual cost is $1,825. If she smokes steadily for 15 years, the total cost is at least $27,375. But many people smoke heavily for 30 years, and Stephanie does too, which brings the total cost to $54,750.

> *"One thousand Americans stop smoking every day - by dying."*
> *– Unknown*

Now let's see how Stephanie's life would be different if she invested her money wisely instead of buying cigarettes with it.

Spending $5 a day for cigarettes costs $150 each month. If Stephanie invested this amount every month at a return rate of 10 percent return, at the end of 30 years her investment would be worth approximately $310,000. And if Stephanie were really smart and invested $75 every two weeks instead of $150 at the end of each month, after 30 years her investment would be valued at almost $340,000. That's a lot of money!

But the huge financial cost of smoking isn't limited to the cost of the cigarettes themselves. Medical and life insurance premiums are higher for smokers (almost double), and smokers tend to replace clothes and furniture more often because these items are damaged by smoke and cigarette burns.

As demonstrated, smoking can be a financial disaster.

Non-financial costs of smoking

I think that it's also important to mention the non-financial impact that smoking has on a person. There are more important things in life than money, and health is definitely on top of that list.

Both my parents were smokers and when they started smoking in the 60s or 70s, the negative health impacts back then were not yet known. Nowadays however, we know that smoking increases life-threatening diseases like lung cancer, heart attacks, and strokes. According to the Medcentral Health System organization in Ohio, someone who smokes heavily (greater than one pack per day) at age 25 can expect to live a full 25 years less than a non-smoker. That's a heavy non-financial price to pay for smoking.

But there are other non-financial benefits to not smoking. For example, if a cigarette takes 5 minutes to smoke and a person smokes 20 a day, someone who doesn't smoke has the benefit of enjoying an extra hour and a half each day compared to his smoking counterpart. A lot can be done with this extra time and it doesn't even take into consideration the time it takes to go buy the cigarettes, searching for lighters, and the time spent emptying ashtrays.

Then there's the taste of food. Food tastes better when a person doesn't smoke because their taste buds aren't affected like a smoker's are. I enjoy my food way too much to want to give it up for a cigarette, which is tasteless. Another downside to smoking involves running out of breath quickly when playing sports and more wrinkles which make you look older. Again, none of which are worth spending money on.

> *"A cigar has a fire at one end and a fool at the other."*
> *– Horace Greely*

Time to act

If you're a smoker, you really should consider quitting. Use the money you save each day to pay off your debt. If you don't have any debts, then invest your cigarette money to earn interest and dividends. Think about what else you could use that money for. You can take nice vacations, purchase a home, or get that car you've always dreamed of. You'll also feel more energetic, and will be able to jump for joy each month as you watch your wallet get fatter from the cost savings of no longer smoking.

If you don't smoke then pretend that you do. But instead of spending $5 each day on cigarettes, invest the money in shares, mutual funds, or bonds. By doing so, you are making your money work for you since these investments will generate passive income for you to enjoy over the remaining years of your life.

Use save to pay

Free is a very powerful word that is used everywhere in advertising. Free sample. Buy two and get one free. Sign up and you get 'something' for free. *Free* is a great advertising tool that gets everyone's attention. It makes us want to act fast before we miss out because anything free is a great deal!

Sadly, most things in life are not free. But I've come up with a way to make things appear to be free. I use what I call my *save to pay* strategies. The formula is very simple—I save my money instead of spending it, and I use the income that my savings generate to buy the things I want.

As I mentioned earlier, I think that bank and ATM fees are unfair. But with my save to pay formula, I reduced my annual bank charges from $700 to zero.

Let me explain. At one point my bank was paying an estimated 7 percent in dividends on its stocks. Working backwards, I calculated that if I was to invest $10,000 in bank shares (which I then did), I would gain annual dividend income of approximately $700. In effect, this eliminates my annual bank charges. The bank pays me $700 in dividends each year, and I turn around and pay it back to them in bank service charges. I'm using the money I get from them to pay off their fees.

Here's another save to pay example—one that has a very beneficial, ongoing effect on my life. When I worked for an accounting firm, my average annual bonus was $7,000. The first year, I used this bonus wisely to pay down my credit card debts. By the second year I was no longer in debt, so I decided to spend my bonus on traveling. But I didn't run out and buy a vacation package right away. Instead, I

> *"All days are not same. Save for a rainy day. When you don't work, savings will work for you."*
> *- M.K. Soni*

came up with a save to pay strategy for my vacations. I decided that I wanted to invest my bonuses in a "travel fund" and use the income from this fund towards my traveling costs in future years.

I did the math to see if it would work out, and discovered that the numbers were very promising. I determined that a good vacation costs an average of about $3,500. I would be investing $7,000 per year—my bonuses—into my travel fund, which had a return rate of 10 percent. Thus, in the first year, I could take a $3,500 trip but I would only have to pay $2,800 out of my regular bank account, because the interest from my travel fund would cover the remaining $700. In the second year, for the $3,500 trip I would only need $2,100 from my bank account, because the travel fund interest would cover the remaining $1,400 (I would have invested another $7,000 in year 2). As the years went on, the travel fund would cover a larger portion of each trip, until finally in the fifth year the interest from my travel fund would cover the entire cost of the trip. Thus, over the five-year period, I would need my bank account to cover a total of $7,000 of traveling costs. By investing wisely every year for five years, I would reduce the cost of my first five vacations from $17,500 to only $7,000. That's a 60 percent cost reduction, which is fantastic.

This table may clarify how the plan worked in those first five years:

Year	Bonus Investment	Cumulative Investment	Rate of Return	Travel Cost	Investment Income	Net Travel Cost
1	$ 7,000	$ 7,000	10%	$ 3,500	$ 700	$ 2,800
2	7,000	14,000	10%	3,500	1,400	$ 2,100
3	7,000	21,000	10%	3,500	2,100	$ 1,400
4	7,000	28,000	10%	3,500	2,800	$ 700
5	7,000	35,000	10%	3,500	3,500	$ -
	Totals over 5 years			$ 17,500	$ 10,500	$ 7,000
				(A)	(B)	(A-B)

As the table clearly shows, after the first five years, I wouldn't need to invest any more money into the travel fund. By that time, the annual interest I earned from the fund would be $3,500, which meant that from then on I could take a vacation every year without having to withdraw *any* money from my bank account!

Of course, this plan would only work if I had the discipline to put my annual $7,000 bonuses into my travel fund for five years in a row rather than spending them, and if I resisted the temptation to dip into my travel fund to pay for anything other than my annual trips.

I was able to do this, and as long as my travel fund keeps earning 10 percent interest per year, I'm set for free travel throughout my life. The investment income I get from my travel fund continues to pay for my vacations, and the principal that I invested, the $35,000, remains untouched.

I have only made one change to this travel fund strategy over the years—when I got married, I doubled my investment in the fund so that it would cover my wife's trips as well. In the future, I may need to increase my principal investment again by a small fraction to keep up with increases in airline, hotel, and other traveling costs.

> *"Make all you can, save all you can, give all you can."*
> *– John Wesley*

Next time you get a bonus—or a pay raise—consider investing the money instead of spending it. The more you save and invest, the more investment income you'll generate, and the more things you can buy with it.

Prepare your own *pay to save* strategies to help you along your road to success. Give it a shot and see how it works out for you.

Do things yourself

Over the last ten years, I've been investing some of my money in bonds, stocks, and mutual funds. A university friend was my financial advisor, and he did all the trading for me. I can't complain about his service, but I found that

I was paying him a lot of commission fees. There were times when all my profits were swallowed up by his commissions, so I started looking for alternatives. I bought books about how to invest, what to invest in, and how to become rich. Then I signed up for online investing with my bank. Gradually, I started to invest on my own using the tips and tools I learned from the books I read. I've been fortunate that most of my investments have done well, and I've saved a lot of money on transaction fees by doing the buying and selling myself. I now pay transaction fees as low as $9.95, which is significantly lower than what I was paying my financial advisor. All it took was a few books to learn how things worked, and off I went to do things on my own and save money.

After starting my accounting business, I wanted to incorporate. I talked to some accountants, lawyers, and paralegals about incorporating, and discovered that the average cost was about $1,200. I thought, "How difficult could it be for me to fill out a few incorporation forms?" So, I did some research on how to incorporate, downloaded the forms I needed online, filled them out, and submitted them with my payment. Within a few days, I had my corporation papers. It only cost me $250 to do it on my own, which saved me close to a thousand dollars. Ironically, I've turned this experience into a money maker—I now charge my clients $1,200 to incorporate companies for them.

A few years ago I wanted to buy a digital camera. I went to an electronics store but came out empty handed because I realized that the salesperson was just saying anything to get me to buy a camera—any camera. When I got home, I got onto the Internet to do some research myself. I read many customer reviews on different cameras and I checked out *Consumer Reports* magazine. By then I knew exactly which camera I wanted, and I went back to the store and bought it. By doing the research myself, I saved a bit of money and saved myself the disappointment of purchasing an unsatisfying camera.

My point is that it pays to take the time to understand how things work. If you rush into things you may not get the best deal. The best way to learn how to do things on your own are by reading books and magazines, talking to people that have done it themselves, and using the Internet.

> *"Real knowledge is to know the extent of one's ignorance."*
> *– Confucius*

The Internet is full of free, useful information. The satisfaction you'll feel from getting things done by yourself will be very rewarding monetarily and emotionally. Each task you accomplish on your own will be a success.

Chapter 7

USE POSITIVE RELATIONSHIPS TO ACHIEVE SUCCESS

In this section you will learn that:

✓ The more positive relationships you have, the more powerful you will be in achieving success.

✓ The "little guys" are actually the "big guys."

✓ You must wag your tail like a dog to make friends.

✓ Acknowledging your mistakes helps you gain the trust of the people around you.

I n this chapter, I'll be sharing with you some of the approaches I take to build and maintain positive, cooperative relationships with the people around me.

While it's true that no one else will hand you success on a platter, it is also true that having good relationships with other people can help you on every step of your way to success.

Put in its crudest terms, having cooperative relationships with other people means that you have some influence over them. But life is all about giving and receiving, which means that cooperation is a two-way street. People who have built positive relationships with others are much more likely to receive—and give—information, advice, time, encouragement and favors

> *"Each friend represents a world in us, a world possibly not born until they arrive, and it is only by this meeting that a new world is born."*
> *– Anais Nin*

than people who believe that relationships can't help them lead successful lives.

The principle of give and take is a very important one. Every time someone does a favor for me, I try to give something in return when I can. And whenever someone asks me for a favor, I always say yes—but I don't expect anything specific in return. I have learned that the vast majority of people will remember the favor I have done them, and will eventually be willing and able to help me in some way.

There are many books available on the importance of networking in your work life. My approach expands on that idea in two ways. First, my definition of a cooperative relationship goes beyond the "meet and greet" approach that many supporters of networking promote. Second, since life success is more than just work or career success, I believe it is crucial to develop cooperative relationships with others in all the areas of your life—your work, your friends, your extended family, your community activities, your hobbies, and so on.

I have found that in order to develop a positive relationship with someone, six criteria must be met. The first and most important is that a person must like you. If he or she doesn't like you, then forget it—you won't be able to build the kind of mutually beneficial relationship with them that I'm talking about. Getting someone to like you is the backbone of having a good relationship with them. Without it you're wasting your time. Once you know that this backbone is in place, then you can start to nurture a cooperative relationship with that person by working towards meeting the other five criteria.

Ideally, the six components of a cooperative relationship are that the other person:

1. knows and likes you.

2. knows that you're understanding.

3. trusts you.

4. feels that you care about them.

5. knows that you're sincere and honest with them.

6. sees you as an equal, and knows that you see them as an equal too.

The more of the above criteria that you can meet, the stronger your influence is because most people will have a soft spot for you. And with that soft spot, they'll be willing to go out of their way to help you if you need it. When they like you and feel completely comfortable trusting you, they will open up their own networks of influences, which you'll eventually be able to access as well.

The more positive relationships I have, the more "powerful" I am. Having large networks in all areas of my life definitely helps me on my road to success, which is why I'm always trying to strengthen my relationships with people I already know, as well as build new relationships to turn more strangers into friends.

> *"Do good to your friends to keep them, to your enemies to win them."*
> *– Benjamin Franklin*

Here are some of the techniques I use to build my networks. These techniques have played a big part in my achievement of success.

Discover their passion

I once had a contract in which I was to interview key personnel at the client company to gather the information I needed to be able to perform my work. I spent two months interviewing people in the organization, and everything had gone well. My next step was to meet with a tax manager to discuss my work to make sure that my findings were correct.

This is where I hit a roadblock—the manager kept brushing me off and wouldn't agree to meet. Weeks went by, and as desperation started kicking in, I became more pushy with him. But my pushiness only agitated the manager, to the point that he wouldn't answer my emails or return my calls. I was running out of options, and I was starting to look bad professionally because I wasn't getting my work done on schedule.

I finally decided to drop by his office, and promised myself that I wouldn't leave until I got the information I needed from him. When I got there he was in a meeting, so I stuck around to wait for him. I noticed that he had medals hung on his office walls and trophies on his shelves—he had won a number of cycling events. Then I noticed a few bicycle magazines lying around in the waiting room.

When the tax manager returned to his office, he found me waiting for him with a magazine in my hands. He didn't look happy to see me, so I quickly spoke before he did. I said, "I didn't know you were into cycling. I'm really impressed!" He was silent for a bit before asking me why I found that impressive. I replied, "I'm impressed because you've got a great position in the company, you're a hardworking individual, married with two kids, and with all those responsibilities you're still able to make time for yourself to win cycling medals. How do you do it? You make a great role model, not only for someone like me, but for many other professionals who are drowning in their careers."

His facial expression changed to reveal a gentler person. He invited me into his office to tell me about his cycling pastime. He told me all about his cycling routines and tours, the different types of bicycles available, and other cycling-related things. He continued to tell me about his dream to cycle in the Tour de France and about how his children were beginning to show some

> *"If you don't like something change it; if you can't change it, change the way you think about it."*
> *– Mary Engelbreit*

interest in cycling. We had a very pleasant conversation about cycling for almost an hour before he looked at me and said, "How can I help you?" I was still buzzing from how friendly he'd become and how it came so unexpectedly.

I had discovered his passion for bicycling, and as a result this man had completely changed his manner towards me. The fact that I was listening to him and asking questions kept him going and going. In all honesty, I wasn't very interested in what he was saying but I didn't want to cut him off or stop him because he seemed so pleased and excited to talk about it.

My discovery of his passion became my ticket to his cooperation. After that meeting, I had my work wrapped up within two weeks. I had to see him twice more and had absolutely no problems setting up these meetings with him. I started off each meeting asking him if and where he biked over the weekend, and the meetings ended with me getting all the information I needed.

People love talking about themselves and their passions, and they connect very quickly with others who share the same interests. Here are the steps to discovering another person's passion:

1. Become an explorer. Pay attention to the pictures and objects that the person keeps around them. Most people who have hobbies generally show some signs about them close by. When I think that I've discovered a passion, I test it out. For example, if I see baby pictures, I start a conversation by saying "Awww, she's adorable. How old is she?" If I see the spark in the eyes of that person, then I know I've discovered one of their passions.

2. Be a good listener. Once you get them talking about their passion, listen to every word they're saying and don't interrupt with your own opinions or experiences. Let the person talking to you believe and feel that you're interested in every word that they say. Without the proper listening skills, you won't be able to pick up the information you need to move on to the next technique.

3. Ask questions that directly relate to what the person is talking about. Your goal is to show that you seem interested in every word the person is saying. I don't know about you, but I love it when I meet new people who ask me questions about myself, my work, my hobbies and so forth. It's a nice feeling to know that someone is interested in hearing what I have to say.

4. Remember what the person says. If you need to write things down to remember them, go ahead and do that. Sometimes when a person is telling me about her children, the first thing I do when the conversation is over is quickly write down the names and ages of the children so I don't forget them. On a day when I know that I'll be seeing her again, I go back to my notes to remember their names and I ask her, by name, how they are doing. You'll see how people are easily pleased and impressed when you remember personal things about them, especially when it involves something they care deeply about.

5. Don't let it go. From time to time, bring up the subject of their passion. This will score you big points because each time you bring it up will be a reminder to that person of what a great person you are.

With these pointers in hand, it's your turn to start discovering people's passions. Don't forget to bring it up from time to time to show that you were listening. This will score you big points as they will feel that you're genuinely interested in them.

Treat everyone with equal respect

One year while working at the accounting firm, I was involved in the annual process to recruit new university graduates. The recruitment team was made up of over 20 people who held a wide range of positions— basically, we were a mix of juniors, seniors, managers, and

> *"The quality of your life is the quality of your relationships."*
> *– Anthony Robbins*

partners. We put up information kiosks at the universities, held cocktail parties and office tours for students, and eventually conducted the interviews.

As the process began, I noticed that many students thought that if they made a good impression on a partner or a manager, it would be easier for them to get a job with the company. As a result, many students spent most of their time meeting and talking to partners and managers and they ignored what I consider the "little guys"—the people who don't have prestigious titles, and who many people assume don't have any power or influence in their company.

But this assumption was incorrect. Everyone on the recruiting team was considered equal, and after each event we had a team meeting to discuss each student. If anybody on the team said, "I don't know who you're talking about" or "I didn't get to meet this person," then the candidate lost some points. And guess what? Many candidates lost points because they never took the time to introduce themselves to the more junior members of the team, such as myself. I was a 'little guy' during this process, but I actually felt like one of the 'big boys' because I had a big say in the granting of an interview.

This experience, along with many others, taught me never to ignore the little guys because the reality is these people do have some influential power in an organization. These are the people who work the hardest to keep the company going, and executives know that without them, the company wouldn't exist. So remember that employees who you perceive to be junior, such as a salesperson in a shoe store, may be a very important person to establish a relationship with (to get a discount, for example!).

When I became a new senior at the accounting firm, I wasn't a little guy anymore, but I made it a point to make alliances with the juniors who reported to me. I made sure to treat each one of them well, and in return they worked harder and longer, which made my job easier. Because we had such a positive relationship, they didn't want to let me down. In return, I made sure I was always there for them and gave them the guidance they needed to do their jobs successfully. From time to time, I would high-five them and tell them how much I loved working with them. Truly, all my teams were great and produced very good results.

It didn't take too long for the word to spread among the junior staff that "Pat is fun to work with." The senior managers realized that many juniors were asking to be on my teams, and that my teams always produced great results. This eventually led to me getting another promotion and salary increase. Treating the little guys well had paid off for me.

Here's another example: At one point, my fax line at the office wasn't working, so I couldn't send or receive faxes. When the phone company technician arrived to fix it, I greeted him with a smile and was friendly to him. While he was hard at work, I offered him a snack and something to drink as an appreciation for his efforts. He found that the problem was not my phone line but my fax machine. Since the problem was considered to be my fault and not the phone company's, I would have to pay for the $140 service call. But I paid nothing! The technician said that he was thankful for my hospitality, so he wrote up the service call as a burnt fuse on the phone panel.

I did the same thing at home with the cable guy, and even offered to hold his ladder as he worked. He gave me 30 additional channels for free!

Everyone has the potential to help you out if you leave a good impression on them. Make friends and you'll start to realize that these little guys will take extra steps to please you and save you money here and there. You'll quickly learn that the reality is that the "little guys" are actually the "big guys."

Be a dog

Who's a dog? Well not to be insulting or anything, but *you* should be a dog. Dogs are wonderful animals who can teach us lots of great lessons, such as:

Dogs give people a big welcome. Every time I come home my dog, Pixie, gives me a big welcome as if she hadn't seen me in 15 years. She runs to me with her tail wagging furiously, jumping up and down, running in circles, and barking in excitement. Her greeting is so genuine it makes me feel like I'm the most important person in the world. She never

> "*I think dogs are the most amazing creatures; they give unconditional love. For me they are the role model for being alive.*"
> – *Gilda Radner*

fails to lift my mood, no matter how hard a day I've had. But this behaviour is not just limited to my dog. One of my best friend's dog used to get so excited when greeting people that she would uncontrollably urinate from her happiness. Now that's what I consider very happy!

Any person that is good at greeting others can make friends easily, because it makes people feel special and appreciated. That's why I try to greet everyone just as a dog does, without the urination of course! In my work life, that means always greeting colleagues and clients with a smile and good eye contact. In my personal life, I pretend that I haven't seen my friends in 15 years, and add a big hug.

Dogs don't stand in front of the door and bark "hi" to everyone. They run frantically from person to person, making sure they don't miss anyone. In other words, they don't show any favorites and they make everyone in the room feel special. I try to do the same by taking the time to greet everyone individually.

When I'm at a social gathering where I don't know everyone, I try not to ignore the new faces because I know a dog wouldn't. I introduce myself to the people that I don't know by saying, "Hi, I'm Patrick. It's nice to meet you." I don't wait until someone introduces me because that just makes things more awkward. It also gives the impression that the people I don't know are less important as the people I already know. Dogs greet strangers just as excitedly as someone they already know, so you should do the same.

It's important to greet strangers because first impressions last forever. If the first impression of you is a good one, people will take a liking to you from the very beginning. The more someone likes you, the more cooperative a relationship you'll be able to build with them. And the sooner they realize they like you, the easier it is to gain their trust.

Dogs don't hold grudges. If I yell at my dog, minutes later she is licking me and wanting to play. She never gives me the cold shoulder because she forgives and forgets, and everything goes back to normal. This is an attitude that I try to maintain.

I generally avoid fights and arguments but if I do find myself in one, my dog instincts kick in. I try to bring my relationship with that person back to how it was in the beginning. I admit it's not always easy to forget, but I always manage to at least forgive. I try not to hold a grudge and revenge is *never* an option. If you're the type to hold a grudge and aim for revenge, then the path forward becomes so much harder. Grudges only result in hate, and hate can lead to distrust and fewer friends. Sometimes you have to swallow your pride and find the power within yourself to start wagging your tail again for the sake of maintaining a good relationship with the people who may help you feel and become successful.

> *"A dog can express more with his tail in seconds than his owner can express with his tongue in hours."*
> *– Unknown*

Now that you know that you're supposed to be a dog, start acting like one and see how quickly you start to make friends. Who knows, *you* may become man's best friend.

The power of "I'm sorry"

Part of showing sincerity and honesty is being able to admit when you're wrong. I do this simply by saying "I'm sorry."

We've all made mistakes and poor decisions in our lives. There's nothing wrong with that—it's part of being human. But it is wrong when we don't step forward to take responsibility for our mistakes. Jesus told us to love one another, not blame each other. So when I do something wrong, I never hesitate to apologize.

Refusing to take ownership of your errors doesn't help you build good relationships. Instead, it creates bad vibes and enemies, which you should avoid doing at all costs. The moment you're perceived as being dishonest or insincere, it will become almost impossible for anyone to trust you.

In 2009, while my wife was going through her chemotherapy treatments, I had a lot on my plate. The constant running around to medical appointments was physically tiring, and I wasn't getting enough sleep. I was worried about my wife's well-being, and the work piling up on my desk every day was adding to my stress. Every day was a struggle, but I had my priorities straight—I was by my wife's side for every appointment and every treatment.

During this difficult period, I completely forgot to file a government form for one of my clients. As a result of my negligence, she received a notice saying she had to pay penalty and interest charges. In my 4 years of dealing with this client, I had never missed a government deadline and I was disappointed in myself for forgetting.

When my client told me the news, I had two options. I could have pretended that I *did* file the form on time, and blamed the government office for losing the form or forgetting to process it. Or, I could tell my client the truth, which would make me look bad and could result in my losing her as a client.

I opted to tell her the truth and apologized for the inconvenience and anxiety it had caused her. I also offered to pay the charges myself. I didn't mention my wife's situation because it wasn't really relevant—I had made a mistake, end of story.

My client didn't get angry with me. On the contrary, she appreciated my apology because it demonstrated honesty. She decided to pay for the penalty charges herself, which was very nice of her, but I couldn't accept her paying for

> *"Never ruin an apology with an excuse."*
> *– Kimberly Johnson*

my mistake. I quickly phoned the government office to explain the situation and to tell them that I would be the one paying the charges, not my client. I admitted my responsibility to them and apologized. Guess what? They reversed the charges because they appreciated my honesty. That's how powerful saying "I'm sorry" is.

Apologizing and taking responsibility go hand in hand with what I said in Chapter 4 about not playing the blame game. Nothing good comes from blaming others, so always be sincere and apologize for your mistakes. Admit when you've done wrong, because it takes a strong, confident person to admit to making a mistake. Acknowledging your mistakes says a lot about you and helps you gain the trust of the people around you.

If you don't already use the above techniques to develop and maintain positive, cooperative relationships with the people around you, start using them now. I'm sure you'll find that it's very rewarding, and that they become very important tools in helping you achieve your success. I hope you make many new friends on your road to success.

Chapter 8

HOW TO STAY ON YOUR ROAD TO SUCCESS

In this section you will learn that:

✓   Performance indicators are necessary to let you know when you achieve success.

✓   Fear is normal as long as it doesn't consume you and prevent you from achieving your goals and successes.

L et's think back to that road trip across Europe. Say you've been driving for many hours, and you're wondering how you're doing. Are you on track to reach your destination, your success?

Measuring your progress on a road trip is fairly simple. Are you on schedule? Are you still on the right road? Are you heading in the right direction? But how do you measure your progress on your roadmaps to success? As I explained in Chapter 3, I develop roadmaps and detailed plans for each aspect of my life.

These detailed plans are, in effect, lists of goals. I measure my success by checking whether I am achieving my goals in the timeframe I set up. For example,

▶ I have a goal to spend quality time with my wife. I consider this goal to be achieved when I consistently spend at least a few hours each day with her, talking and doing the things that we enjoy together.

▶ I have a goal to meet my clients' expectations. I consider this goal to be achieved when I've correctly performed all my tasks within the required deadlines. If I don't meet all my deadlines, then I know that I've failed.

▶ My wife and I value spending time with our families. Our standard of success is visiting with them at least once every ten days. If we go more than ten days without seeing them, we invite them over or visit them.

The examples above involve clearly defined goals that I have set. But in some cases, I compare my "success performance" to something or someone else. For example,

▶ I compare many things I achieve against statistics on how the average person doing the same task performs. When I do better than the average, I feel good and successful. I started using this approach when I was in school—I compared my grades to the class average. Success was earning a grade equal to or above the class average. If I scored below the class average, I knew I had to work harder to achieve success on the next exam.

▶ Sometimes I compare the old to the new. When I bought my latest car, I compared it to my previous one. I was very pleased that it drove better, it had more features, it was more comfortable, and my lease payments were within my budget. Therefore, that was a successful purchase.

▶ Sometimes I look at general trends in my performance. With my business, I look at my bottom line every month, quarter and year to see if I made or lost money. At the very least, I need to have made a profit to call that month, quarter or year a success. But I also compare this month to last month, or this quarter to last quarter, to see if my income is on a general upward trend.

These are just a few examples. With other goals, I compare my success performance against a quality measure, my age, a target date, and even a target time.

A success story

Since I was 18, one of my goals in life was to try the $500 slot machine at the Montreal Casino. I never expected to win, and I'm not a gambler, but I wanted to be able to afford to lose a $500 coin in less than ten seconds without really caring. I knew that once I was able to do that, I would have achieved enough wealth to feel successful financially. Playing that machine was my measurement of success.

For 14 years, my friend and I talked about the day when we'd be successful enough to fulfil our dream. I thought about it often, and visualized dropping in one coin and pulling once, just to be able to say "I did it; I played the machine." If by chance I actually won something, that would be an unexpected bonus.

Just before I turned 32, my friend and I decided that the time had come to achieve our dream. We were business partners and our company was doing well, so the time was right. We went out for dinner with our wives and headed over to the casino. Just as we had always talked about and visualized, we walked into the VIP section of the casino.

At the entrance of the room, there were leather couches and nice big towels to wash our hands. The room was very private, and we were the only ones there. I felt like a million dollars just being in that room. This was the feeling that I had longed for all these years, and it was even better than I had imagined it to be. When we dropped the coin into the machine, my adrenaline was

> *"Life consists not in holding good cards but in playing those you hold well."*
> *– Josh Billings*

pumping—not because I was nervous about losing $500, but because I was excited that I had finally achieved this milestone. Seconds later, we lost the money. But we were happy, both smiling with pride. What a feeling—I felt successful!

When I share this experience with friends and colleagues, most people think I was crazy. But this is where everyone is wrong—I didn't lose anything. I had set myself a goal and then worked towards it for 14 years. Paying $500 for a ten-second thrill to feel successful and achieve a dream was worth every penny. I felt like a winner and was proud of it. It was only through this experience that I knew I had achieved one of my financial successes.

Measuring your success

Get out your roadmaps, timelines, detailed plans, and any other success tools you use. Do all of your interim and final goals, no matter how small or how large, have measurable performance indicators? If not, you need to establish them now.

While thinking of your measurement factors, keep the follow points in mind:

1. Stay true to yourself. What will it take for *you* to feel successful? Remember that you need to satisfy yourself, not the people around you. Define your performance indicators for yourself—only

you know what it will take for you to feel satisfied and successful.

2. Be realistic. If you're expecting an annual salary of three million dollars from a marketing position that pays only $45,000, you're setting yourself up for a miserable life. Your measurement should be realistic and something within your reach.

3. Be patient. Happiness is the key to a successful life, but happiness can't always be achieved quickly. For most people, it takes time to achieve complete happiness. As long as you know what it takes to feel happy, then you'll know the challenges you need to conquer to feel happiness in your success.

4. Set deadlines. Deadlines are all around us in our daily lives, and many people dislike and dread them. But to achieve complete success, you have to put deadlines on yourself in everything you do.

5. Don't give up. Nothing in life is perfect and not everything goes according to plan. Failure to achieve a goal shouldn't be the end. Instead, it should be a lesson to help you tackle the task again. Don't give up, and always try to have an alternative plan in case something goes wrong.

When all your performance indicators are in place, review them regularly to make sure you're still on the right road. If you have taken a wrong turn anywhere, make the necessary corrections to get yourself back on track as quickly as possible. The longer you keep going in the wrong direction, the harder it will be to find your way back to the right road.

Are you afraid of success?

I know that it sounds unbelievable but, unfortunately, many people fear success—they are afraid to deal with the outcomes of success. Many of these people are not consciously aware of their fear, so they are not able to take the appropriate measures needed to conquer this fear.

Where does the fear of success come from? Generally, fear is something we pick up from the adults and media around us when we're children. But most of our fears are subconscious, and thus deeply hidden from even ourselves. You may *think* that you

> *"You always pass failure on the way to success."*
> *– Mickey Rooney*

want to be successful, but in the back of your mind you may believe that you don't deserve it, or that success will bring lifestyle changes that you don't want.

Parents who feel successful are more likely to fill their children with confidence, making them feel important and special, while teaching them that they deserve success and can achieve anything they want in life. Parents that are not satisfied with their lives are more likely to fill their children with self-doubt and feelings of being undeserving. Whether these teachings are done directly or indirectly, the subconscious mind picks it up and stores it in our brains without our conscious knowledge. As we grow older, these teachings become our fears.

The biggest challenge is identifying your fears. To identify mine, I use the visualization techniques that I described in Chapter 5 before I begin new commitments and projects. I start by asking myself, "What will happen if I succeed?" and try to play it all out in my head. But I don't picture what I *hope* will happen, because I want to be realistic and true to myself. Instead, I visualize what I think will *really* happen, and how my success in this area will affect my life—what changes it will bring to me and my family.

This takes more than just a few minutes. You need to think hard about it, playing it over and over in your mind. By doing this, you'll start to realize what fears are hiding deep inside you—the fears that are blocking you from truly achieving your success.

Let me share with you some of the fears I had to overcome when I decided to start my own accounting practice.

1. My relationships might suffer. Starting a business is hard work and very time consuming, so I was worried about not being able to spend time with my wife. What would happen to our relationship? Could it hit a point where divorce becomes the

best solution? Then there were my family and friends—might they be jealous of my success and treat me differently? Could they try to use me for my money?

2. My business might take up all my time. Would I still be able to find the time to enjoy volunteering, traveling, exercising, and watching movies?

3. Starting a business requires money. I needed to rent an office, hire employees, buy computers and office equipment, and so on. That's a big investment, especially when I had no guarantee that I would succeed. Would I be able to support myself financially if the accounting practice didn't work out?

By getting these fears out in the open before I opened my business, I had the opportunity to deal with these fears until I was comfortable enough that they would not make me fail. I thought each fear through and dealt with each one. Once I had addressed each fear, I wasn't afraid anymore

> *"Fear of failure must never be a reason not to try something."*
> *– Frederick Smith*

and felt ready and confident with my decision to move forward.

Some of the most common fears linked to success are listed below. Instead of letting these fears scare you, identify and deal with them sooner rather than later.

▶ **Success will lead to loneliness:** Some men believe that success will mean working long hours, which means neglecting their wives and children, which in turn could result in divorce. Some women believe that success will make them unlovable and intimidating to men.

▶ **Success will lead to envy:** This is a reality we cannot ignore. Many people want what others have, and the more success a person achieves, the more envious are that person's friends, neighbors, and colleagues.

▶ **I'm not good enough for success:** This belief can result from many things, such as having negative parents and not having a college degree. With this belief often comes "I don't deserve success."

▶ **Success will change my lifestyle:** Some people fear that the changes that come with success will actually make life less enjoyable. They believe that they will have less time to, for example, watch television, surf the Internet, spend time with their family, and so on.

▶ **Success is too expensive:** There's a cost to everything, and success is not an exception. Sometimes, to make money you have to spend money, and some may feel that the costs (of starting a new business, for example) are too high.

Others fear that a divorce caused by success will result in legal costs. Even such simple successes as losing weight may be seen as being expensive because of the cost of special foods and having to purchase a new wardrobe.

▶ **I won't be able to control everything that happens:** One of my mottos is "If you can't control it then you shouldn't fear or worry about it." Too many people in North America spend too much time fearing the uncontrollable, which results in unhealthy stress and worry. You may fear death, but since there's nothing you can do to avoid it, there's no point wasting your time worrying about it. Concentrate on living your life instead. You may fear being in a car or plane crash, but don't let that stop you from going to places where you need or want to go.

I'm not saying that fearing something is wrong. The point I'm trying to make is that feeling scared or worried is normal, as long as this fear does not consume you and prevent you from achieving your goals and success. Being worried and stressed out about things that you have no control over will interfere with your enjoyment of life. It will affect you

> *"FEAR is an acronym in the English language for "False Evidence Appearing Real."*
> *– Neale Donald Walsch*

mentally and physically, and you still won't be able to control the uncontrollable, so what's the point? There is no point so don't let yourself worry over something you have no control over, or at least try not to let it bother you. Instead, get involved in other activities to get it off your mind. If you're waiting to hear from your doctor following a blood test, go out and do something fun that will take your mind off your worries. Whether you decide to stay home and stress over your results or go out and enjoy a movie, your test results will be the same in the end. Worrying leads to stress that affects our health, which in turn can reduce the length of your life. By worrying about dying, for example, we are actually bringing ourselves closer to death! Life is precious and too short to waste on worry.

Conquering the fear of success

My grandmother has always been my inspiration whenever I find myself facing a fear. 30 years ago, she was in an airplane that suddenly nosedived more than 10,000 feet. As anyone could imagine, she has developed a fear of flying after that experience, but instead of allowing the fear to consume her, she learnt to deal with it. She continuously brushes her fear aside and has been able to enjoy her life through frequent travelling. She is a great example which shows that fear should never stop in the way. There is a way around everything and fear is not an exception. So whether you have a fear of success or some other fear blocking you in life, you should recognize that fear and find the best way to conquer it.

Here are some approaches that may help you conquer your fears:

1. You have to really want to succeed at whatever you're doing. Without that true desire, the slightest amount of fear will defeat you because, deep inside, you never really wanted that success. That is why it's so important to focus on your own goals rather than the expectations of society and the people around you.

2. As stated above, you can't deal with your fears until you have identified them.

3. Stand up to your fears step by step. Break the task down into a series of small goals. As you achieve each one without dire consequences, this should tip the balance of success in your favor.

4. Promise yourself a reward that's big enough to outweigh your fear. When a reward outweighs your fear, then you will push yourself harder to success.

5. If all else fails, you'll have to accept your fear and just live with it. But try to keep it on the back burner so it doesn't interfere with working towards your success. As you achieve each step along the way, congratulate yourself for working through (or around) your fear.

For some people, fear is very complicated. Look for books and other resources on understanding and eliminating fear—there are lots of them available.

Keep in mind that the biggest failure is not trying to achieve a success that you truly desire. Don't rob yourself of the chance for success because of fear. Stand up to your fear and show it that you're the boss.

Never give up

In the beginning of this book I warned you that you'll encounter many obstacles on your road to success—potholes, closed roads, construction, accidents, detours, and one-way streets. None of these obstacles should discourage you from finding alternative routes, and none of them should be used as an excuse for giving up.

I know that it is sometimes difficult to keep pushing forward, but we always have to look inside ourselves to find the will and the power to continue moving on. Each time I find that I'm faced with something that seems impossible to conquer, I remind myself of what Jesus went through on his way to Calvary. Battered and weak, he carried his own cross on his way to his crucifixion. With the weight

> *"You can have it all. Anything you want you can make it yours."*
> *– Shakira*

of the cross on his shoulders, he fell to the ground several times but, each time, instead of *'giving up'* he *'got back up'*. Knowing that each step he took would lead him closer to his death, he still managed to find the power to stand up again. Imagine that; not even death was strong enough to keep him down! His example carries a very powerful and inspirational message—*no matter what, always rise back up.*

Life was never meant to be easy, so don't let any obstacles get in your way or make you give up. Every time you feel that someone or something has pushed you down, rise back up to the challenge and take another step forward. As long as you never give up, you will never be a failure.

Some final thoughts

Imagine a bank that automatically puts $86,400 into your account every morning. It carries no balance from day to day, allows you to keep no cash balance, and every evening cancels out whatever part of that $86,400 you didn't use during the day. What would you do if you had such a bank account? I'm pretty sure that you would withdraw the whole $86,400 every day so you wouldn't lose a penny of it!

Everyone has a magical bank like this—the bank of time. Every morning, it gives you 86,400 seconds to spend during the day. Every night, it wipes out time you have failed to invest to good purpose. If you fail to use the day's deposit, the loss is yours. There's no going back, and there's no drawing against tomorrow.

Since you are given the same number of seconds every day, you never have "too little" or "too much" time in your life. How you manage your allotment of seconds is decided by you alone. The issue is never not having enough time to do things—it's how badly you want to do them. On your road to success, never forget that time is precious and limited. Why wait to do something tomorrow when it can be done today? Life is too short for us to let it pass us by, so make the best of your life and make sure that you enjoy every second of every day.

> *"Time is our most valuable asset, yet we tend to waste it, kill it, and spend it rather than invest it."*
> *– Jim Rohn*

To date, I have achieved many successes and I'm very proud of myself. But I know that it's not over yet. I still have many years ahead of me, I hope, and I trust that they will bring me more achievements and successes. Achieving success is such a great feeling of accomplishment, and it's so sad that some people are never able to feel that satisfaction. That's why I believe that every person in the world—including you—deserves to feel that they have had a successful life. Only you have the power to achieve your success.

I have written this book to give you some tips and pointers, but the rest is up to you. I wish you the best of luck finding your road to success!

MY CONTACT INFORMATION

I hope this book helped you on your road to finding success. I'd love to hear from you if:

- ▶ You have any comments or suggestions about something you've read.

- ▶ You read something that you liked.

- ▶ If you have a personal inspiring success story you'd like to share.

- ▶ If you disagree with anything I say. Your personal view points are important to me.

I can be reached by email at

patrick@findingyourroadtosuccess.com

I can be reached by post mail at

12354 Granger
Pierrefonds, Quebec
Canada, H9G-2Y8
To the attention of – Patrick Daniel

Website

www.findingyourroadtosuccess.com

QUOTES LISTED THROUGHOUT THIS BOOK

In order of appearance.

1. *"The superior man blames himself. The inferior man blames others."*
   – Don Shula

2. *"It is our attitude at the beginning of a difficult task which, more than anything else, will affect its successful outcome."*
   – William James

3. *"A successful man is one who can lay a firm foundation with the bricks others have thrown at him."*
   – David Brinkley

4. *"Success doesn't come to you. You go to it."*
   – Marva Collins

5. *"Health is the greatest gift, contentment the greatest wealth, faithfulness the best relationship."*
   – Buddha

6. *"Wherever you go, no matter what the weather, always bring your own sunshine."*
   – Anthony J. D'Angelo

7. *"Dream as if you'll live forever, live as if you'll die today."*
    – James Dean

8. *"Don't confuse fame with success. Madonna is one; Helen Keller is the other."*
    – Erma Bombeck

9. *"If your success is not on your own terms, if it looks good to the world but does not feel good in your heart, it is not success at all."*
    – Anna Quindlen

10. *"No matter how far you fall down, you gotta be ready to stand up."*
    – Akon

11. *"Success is a state of mind. If you want success, start thinking of yourself as a success."*
    – Dr. Joyce Brothers

12. *"Let us be thankful for the fools. But for them the rest of us could not succeed."*
    – Mark Twain

13. *"The difference between a successful person and others is not a lack of strength, not a lack of knowledge, but rather in a lack of will."*
    – Vincent T. Lombardi

14. *"Happiness is not by chance, but by choice."*
    – Jim Rohn

15. *"Success is getting what you want. Happiness is wanting what you get."*
   – Dale Carnegie

16. *"Happiness is an attitude. We either make ourselves miserable, or happy and strong. The amount of work is the same."*
   – Francesca Reigler

17. *"Develop success from failures. Discouragement and failure are two of the surest stepping stones to success."*
   – Dale Carnegie

18. *"Success is not the key to happiness. Happiness is the key to success. If you love what you are doing, you will be successful."*
   – Herman Cain

19. *"Know where you are headed, and you will stay on solid ground."*
   – Proverbs 4:26

20. *"Success depends upon previous preparation, and without such preparation there is sure to be failure."*
   – Confucius

21. *"Arriving at one goal is the starting point to another."*
   – John Dewey

22. *"All you need is the plan, the roadmap, and the courage to press on to your destination."*
   – Earl Nightingale

23. *"Every person, all the events of your life are there because you have drawn them there. What you choose to do with them is up to you."*
    – Richard Bach

24. *"A good plan is like a roadmap: it shows the final destination and usually the best way to get there."*
    – H. Stanley Judd

25. *"Don't go around saying the world owes you a living. The world owes you nothing. It was here first."*
    – Mark Twain

26. *"A man can get discouraged many times but he is not a failure until he begins to blame somebody else and stops trying."*
    – John Burroughs

27. *"No one is a failure until they blame somebody else."*
    – Charles "Tremendous" Jones

28. *"If we can really understand the problem, the answer will come out of it, because the answer is not separate from the problem."*
    – Jiddu Krishnamurti

29. *"You know, sometimes bad things happen and you don't understand why and you just have to trust that there's a good reason for it."*
    – Lois *from television sitcom Malcolm in the Middle*

30. *"Things turn out best for the people who make the best of the way things turn out."*
   – Art Linkletter

31. *"Attitude is a little thing that makes a big difference."*
   – Winston Churchill

32. *"God makes everything happen at the right time. Yet none of us ever fully understand all he has done."*
   – Ecclesiastes 3:11

33. *"If you judge people, you have no time to love them."*
   – Mother Teresa

34. *"You know something? As long as we've been here we've believed that, as aliens, we were superior. But what I've realized is that nobody is superior; they're all just different, that's all."*
   – Dick Solomon *from television sitcom 3rd Rock from the Sun*

35. *"Love others as much as you love yourself."*
   – Jesus

36. *"He who gives to the poor will never be in need."*
   – Proverbs 28:27

37. *"Don't judge others and God won't judge you. Don't be hard on others and God won't be hard on you. Forgive others and God will forgive you."*
   –Luke 6:37

38. *"Everything you ask for in prayer will be yours, if you only have faith."*
   – Mark 11:24

39. *"The more we depend on God the more dependable we find He is."*
   – Cliff Richard

40. *"Without God, man neither knows which way to go, nor even understands who he is."*
   – Pope Benedict XVI

41. *"Even though the blame's on you, I will take that blame from you."*
   – Akon

42. *"There's a voice inside you that tells you what you should do."*
   – Alan Rickman

43. *"Do not follow the ideas of others, but learn to listen to the voice within yourself. Your body and mind will become clear and you will realize the unity of all things."*
   – Dogen

44. *"The most important thing is to pretend, as best you can, that something is true."*
   – Mark Fisher

45. *"Success often comes to those who have the aptitude to see way down the road."*
   – Laing Burns, Jr.

46. *"Until I started giving, I never really appreciated how much I have."*
   – **Dick Solomon** *from television sitcom* 3rd Rock from the Sun

47. *"Happiness comes when we test our skills towards some meaningful purpose."*
   – **John Stossel**

48. *"The best way to cheer yourself is to try to cheer someone else up."*
   – **Mark Twain**

49. *"Sometimes you can become rich by being generous, or poor by being greedy."*
   – **Proverbs 11:24**

50. *"Those who think they have no time for bodily exercise will sooner or later have to find time for illness."*
   – **Edward Stanley**

51. *"If your dog is fat, you're not getting enough exercise."*
   – **Unknown**

52. *"To be upset over what you don't have is to waste what you do have."*
   – **Ken S. Keyes, Jr.**

53. *"A banker is a fellow who lends you his umbrella when the sun is shining, but wants it back the minute it begins to rain."*
   – **Mark Twain**

54. *"A budget tells us what we can't afford, but it doesn't keep us from buying it."*
   – William Feather

55. *"Some couples go over their budgets very carefully every month; others just go over them."*
   – Sally Poplin

56. *"The credit card industry is out of control, it's getting away with robbery."*
   – Robert Heady

57. *"You want 21% risk free? Pay off your credit cards."*
   – Andrew Tobias

58. *"Social security, bank account, and credit card numbers aren't just data. In the wrong hands they can wipe out someone's life savings, wreck their credit and cause financial ruin."*
   – Melissa Bean

59. *"One thousand Americans stop smoking every day— by dying."*
   – Unknown

60. *"A cigar has a fire at one end and a fool at the other."*
   – Horace Greely

61. *"All days are not the same. Save for a rainy day. When you don't work, savings will work for you."*
   – M.K. Soni

62. *"Make all you can, save all you can, give all you can."*
 – John Wesley

63. *"Real knowledge is to know the extent of one's ignorance."*
 – Confucius

64. *"Each friend represents a world in us, a world possibly not born until they arrive, and it is only by this meeting that a new world is born."*
 – Anais Nin

65. *"Do good to your friends to keep them, to your enemies to win them."*
 – Benjamin Franklin

66. *"If you don't like something change it; if you can't change it, change the way you think about it."*
 – Mary Engelbreit

67. *"The quality of your life is the quality of your relationships."*
 – Anthony Robbins

68. *"I think dogs are the most amazing creatures; they give unconditional love. For me they are the role model for being alive."*
 – Gilda Radner

69. *"A dog can express more with his tail in seconds than his owner can express with his tongue in hours."*
 – Unknown

70. *"Never ruin an apology with an excuse."*
   – Kimberly Johnson

71. *"Life consists not in holding good cards but in playing those you hold well."*
   – Josh Billings

72. *"You always pass failure on the way to success. "*
   – Mickey Rooney

73. *"Fear of failure must never be a reason not to try something."*
   – Frederick Smith

74. *"FEAR is an acronym in the English language for "False Evidence Appearing Real."*
   – Neale Donald Walsch

75. *"You can have it all. Anything you want you can make it yours."*
   – Shakira

76. *"Time is our most valuable asset, yet we tend to waste it, kill it, and spend it rather than invest it."*
   – Jim Rohn

APPENDIX 1
(Budget template)

INCOME	Budget	Actual	Difference
Wages & Tips	0.00	0.00	-
Interest Income	0.00	0.00	-
Dividends	0.00	0.00	-
Rental Income	0.00	0.00	-
Gifts Received	0.00	0.00	-
Other	0.00	0.00	-
Total INCOME	-	-	-

HOME EXPENSES	Budget	Actual	Difference
Home Mortgage/Rent	0.00	0.00	-
Electricity	0.00	0.00	-
Gas/Oil	0.00	0.00	-
Water/Sewer/Trash	0.00	0.00	-
Phone	0.00	0.00	-
Cable/Satellite	0.00	0.00	-
Internet	0.00	0.00	-
Furnishings/Appliances	0.00	0.00	-
Lawn/Garden	0.00	0.00	-
Alarm	0.00	0.00	-
Maintenance/Improvements	0.00	0.00	-
Property Taxes	0.00	0.00	-
Other	0.00	0.00	-
Total HOME EXPENSES	-	-	-

DAILY LIVING	Budget	Actual	Difference
Groceries	0.00	0.00	-
Clothing	0.00	0.00	-
Dining/Eating Out	0.00	0.00	-
Dry Cleaning	0.00	0.00	-
Salon/Barber	0.00	0.00	-
Other	0.00	0.00	-
Total DAILY LIVING	-	-	-

Appendix 1 – Budget template

CHILDREN	Budget	Actual	Difference
Medical			-
Clothing			-
School Tuition			-
School Lunch			-
School Supplies			-
Babysitting			-
Toys/Games			-
Other			-
Total CHILDREN	-	-	-

TRANSPORTATION	Budget	Actual	Difference
Vehicle Payments			-
Fuel			-
Bus/Taxi/Train Fare			-
Repairs			-
Registration/License			-
Other			-
Total TRANSPORTATION	-	-	-

HEALTH	Budget	Actual	Difference
Doctor/Dentist			-
Medicine/Drugs			-
Health Club Fees			-
Emergency			-
Other			-
Total HEALTH	-	-	-

INSURANCE	Budget	Actual	Difference
Auto			-
Health			-
Home/Rental			-
Life			-
Other			-
Total INSURANCE	-	-	-

Appendix 1 – Budget template

CHARITY/GIFTS	Budget	Actual	Difference
Gifts Given			-
Charitable Donations			-
Religious Donations			-
Other			-
Total CHARITY/GIFTS	-	-	-

ENTERTAINMENT	Budget	Actual	Difference
Videos/DVDs			-
Music			-
Games			-
Rentals			-
Movies/Theater			-
Concerts/Plays			-
Books			-
Hobbies			-
Film/Photos			-
Sports			-
Outdoor Recreation			-
Toys/Gadgets			-
Other			-
Total ENTERTAINMENT	-	-	-

PETS	Budget	Actual	Difference
Food			-
Medical			-
Toys/Supplies			-
Other			-
Total PETS	-	-	-

SUBSCRIPTIONS	Budget	Actual	Difference
Newspaper			-
Magazines			-
Association Memberships			-
Other			-
Total SUBSCRIPTIONS	-	-	-

Appendix 1 – Budget template

VACATION	Budget	Actual	Difference
Travel			-
Lodging			-
Food			-
Rental Car			-
Entertainment			-
Other			-
Total VACATION	-	-	-

MISCELLANEOUS	Budget	Actual	Difference
Bank Fees			-
Postage			-
Other			-
Other			-
Other			-
Other			-
Total MISCELLANEOUS	-	-	-

MONTHLY BUDGET SUMMARY	Budget	Actual	Difference
Total Income	0.00	0.00	0.00
Total Expenses	0.00	0.00	0.00
NET	0.00	0.00	0.00